With Sappho
in the Antipathies

James Harpur is a multi-award-winning poet, novelist and non-fiction writer and a member of Aosdána, the Irish academy of the arts. He was born of an Irish father and a British mother who was raised in Paris. He studied Classics and English at Cambridge University and has taught English in Crete and worked as a lexicographer and freelance writer and reviewer. He has published eight collections of poetry and won many prizes, including the Vincent Buckley Poetry Prize, the UK National Poetry Competition and the Michael Hartnett Poetry Prize. His debut novel, *The Pathless Country*, has won the JG Farrell award and was shortlisted for the 2022 John McGahern Fiction Prize. His work has appeared in national newspapers, including the *Irish Times*, *Examiner*, *Independent*, *Guardian* and *Financial Times*, and he regularly broadcasts on radio, including RTÉ Radio 1, Lyric FM, and BBC Radio 4. He lives in West Cork.

With Sappho
in the Antipathies

JAMES HARPUR

HYBRID
PUBLISHERS

Published by Hybrid Publishers

Melbourne Victoria Australia

© James Harpur 2025

This publication is copyright. Apart from any use as permitted under the
Copyright Act 1968, no part may be reproduced by any process without
prior written permission from the publisher. Requests and inquiries
concerning reproduction should be addressed to
the Publisher, Hybrid Publishers,
PO Box 52, Ormond, Victoria, Australia 3204.
info@hybridpublishers.com.au

www.hybridpublishers.com.au

First published 2025

A catalogue record for this
book is available from the
NATIONAL
LIBRARY   National Library of Australia
OF AUSTRALIA

ISBN: 9781922768391 (p)
ISBN: 9781922768407 (e)

Cover design: Gittus Graphics https://www.gggraphics.com.au/
Typeset in Minion Pro
Back cover photo credit: Dino Ignani

Acknowledgements

A passage of this book first appeared in *Axon,* and I would like to thank the editors Jen Webb and Paul Munden for their help and encouragement. The poem 'Letter to Charles Harpur' is from my book *The White Silhouette* (Carcanet, 2018); 'Origen' is from Oracle Bones (Anvil, 2000); and 'The Perfect Tense' is from *The Examined Life* (Two Rivers Press, 2021), which includes the poems that won the Vincent Buckley Prize. I would like to thank the University of Melbourne and the judges and organisers of the Vincent Buckley Prize, which enabled me to visit Australia; and heartfelt gratitude to the many people in Melbourne and Sydney who made my stay so memorable. I mention many of them by name in the book, but I would like to give special thanks to Kevin, Penelope, Yol and David, and of course Sappho.

*To Kevin Brophy and Penelope Buckley, with great affection
and gratitude*

And in memory of Sappho

It was early on the morning of March the twenty-seventh that I took to the road. There was darkness lingering in the sky, and the moon was still visible, though gradually thinning away.

—Matsuo Bashō, *The Narrow Road to the Deep North*

To see the truth, there must be freedom, and a mind that is conditioned according to a system can never see the truth.

—J. Krishnamurti

Down, down, down … I wonder if I shall fall right through the earth! How funny it'll seem to come out among the people that walk with their heads downward! The Antipathies, I think … but I shall have to ask them what the name of the country is, you know. Please, Ma'am, is this New Zealand or Australia?

—Lewis Carroll, *Alice in Wonderland*

From Cork to the heavens …

I close my eyes and see the full moon hanging low in the pre-dawn sky above the terraced houses of Acton in the west of London. It has the same vanilla glow as the solitary street lamp at the end of the road.

A sudden judder: the moon shatters into a thousand icicles and a seatbelt sign pings fiery red. Turbulence.

A few hours ago I was with my friend Eileen, creeping woozily from her flat at a sacrilegious hour in the morning, already feeling jet-lagged and with museum-aching feet: the click of Eileen's front door lock felt as if it would wake the neighbourhood.

As if suddenly realising how high it is above the clouds, the vast Airbus is trembling all over as it glides like a spaceship to the Antipathies.

I cannot stop myself reflecting on the current conflict in the Middle East and whether over its airspace we'll be mistaken for a bomber and dealt with accordingly. After all, the Russians did shoot down a South Korean passenger plane in the early 1980s. I know this outcome is unlikely. But the fear resists all banishment.

I try to catch the eye of the man next to me. It would be nice to have a distracting chat about something anodyne like the weather or football. But he's hypnotised by a computer game. I swivel my eyes like a weird deep-ocean fish and see that his game involves firing missiles at an aircraft.

Airport farewell:
every hug a rehearsal
for the final take-off?

I take refuge in a misty crystal ball of memory: I see Cork airport in drizzle; I see the pub where I'd had my ritual send-off. A slouch of old friends around a table stacked with empties, having fun by preying on my fears with droll doses of lazy stereotyping. Ian is clutching the bridge of his nose, eyes screwed up: 'Australia! You must be mad. I can't think of a place on the planet I'd rather *not* visit. A friend of mine was in Australia, swimming in the sea, doing the breaststroke, and a big blond Aussie swims up alongside him and says, *angrily*: "Nah, nah, nah—that's not how a bloke swims, mate—breaststroke is for sheilas, you've gotta do the crawl, mate."'

Declan says: 'You'll take one step outside the city limits, just one step, and bang!—a boomerang will get you. Smack round the back of the neck. It only needs one step.' He demonstrates this by letting his head droop brokenly from his neck. I'm expecting a dry laugh, but his lips are set horizontally, razor-blade thin, and the whites of his eyes turn to me with the glitter of a Tarot reader who's just seen the Hanged Man.

Of course there's the usual dull hilarity over redbacks, crocodiles, cane toads, hurricanes, and brutish Australians asking me: 'What the eff's a poet?' Everyone thinks they can do an Australian accent.

Faye introduces a note of sobriety: 'Just remind me. Why exactly are you going?'

She knows I am semi-phobic about flying; hate travel and technology; can't take sunshine; can barely swim; I'm scared of spiders, and shy and introverted. I have perfect qualities for sitting in a room and writing poetry, and never going out; but not for flying to what my friends are depicting as a circle of the Inferno painted by Bosch, after a tooth extraction.

'I won the Vincent Buckley Poetry Prize—named after one of Australia's finest modern poets. The money is to enable me to spend time in Australia.'

'To do what?'

'Write? Meet other poets? Foster cultural relations between Australia and Ireland?'

There is a strange silence. Then everyone reacts as if I've told the best joke in the world.

The plane continues to shudder—or perhaps it's dead still and it's my soul that is shuddering?

I reflect on what Eileen has said about Australia. She spent her youth in Adelaide—her family had arrived there from Glasgow on a 'ten-pound-Pom' ticket—but she left at the earliest opportunity. She remembered her family's first accommodation in a Nissen hut, her convent schooling; and she cited broiling summers, lack of culture and endless materialism and suburbia as the reasons for her departure. But that was Adelaide. That was way back in the late 1960s. People change, countries evolve, surely? She said Melbourne was the best place to go to, followed by Sydney. Luckily, those are my two destinations.

It will be fine. Of course it will be fine. I don't have to interact with Australians if I don't want to—perhaps the odd poet and university administrator. I know that Australia has one of the largest number of fatally poisonous creatures in the world, but … as a non-swimmer I'm unlikely to salsa with a saltwater crocodile or sing to a stinging stonefish (which produces such a shock of pain the mind collapses and you die); I won't be boxing clever with a box jellyfish or swimming with a great white shark or snorkelling into the arms of a blue-ringed octopus. And if I stick to urban areas I'll probably avoid the inland taipan snake (whose venom is strong enough to kill several humans with one bite), the aptly named 'common death adder' and the red-bellied black snake. But I do admit I'll have to be more vigilant at a more micro level: the redback spider, funnel-web spider, paralysis tick, bull ant, and giant centipede could ruin your day, a.k.a. end your life. No, it will be good. Plenty of time to write in solitude and sunshine. A cheeky little latte in a tucked-away café now and again. Mediterranean climate with everyone speaking English and eating fish and chips. Perfect.

> Beyond the aircraft
> the strangest country—
> the setting sun *rising*?

The man next to me is still computer-fixated. I reach up to turn on my reading spotlight and hit the wrong button; an icy beam pinpoints his screen like a death ray, but nothing deflects him from shooting down aircraft. I am equally absorbed—about missing my connection in Dubai, as well as getting from Singapore airport to my hotel for one night. My left brain knows that it's completely simple; my right one's creating nightmare fantasies. The aeroplane to Singapore that has a strange whining noise coming from one of its engines. The Melbourne customs officer who says my visa is invalid and I must go to a detention centre. O my kingdom for a pair of dream-catcher earrings, upgraded to industrial strength to gather up anxieties.

I flick around the in-flight entertainment and find, improbably, a film about Emily Dickinson in Amherst. Emily must be the patron saint of non-travellers, and the conscience of all poets. Her poetry world was the antithesis of that of the modern poet, who must joust in tournaments of literary festivals, workshops, creative writing programs, book launches, and so on. Emily wrote 1,800 poems and published about six of them during her lifetime. Her idea of a book tour was a stroll around her garden, reciting to the marigolds.

The film shows her being intense, witty, acerbic—a virgin wearing white and married to the solitary life. She hardly sets foot outside her soothing Puritan bedroom, yet she leaves it daily in her imagination. How I wish I could swap places with her, at least for the next twenty hours. She said that poets should see the world 'slantwise', a way of perceiving that she shows in her quirky gnomic poems, some of which are used in the film as voice-overs.

I reason, Earth is short—
And Anguish—absolute—
And many hurt,
But what of that?

I reason we could die—
The best Vitality
Cannot excel Decay,
But, what of that?

I reason, that in Heaven—
Somehow, it will be even
Some new equation, given—
But, what of that?

The film reminds me poetry is an affair of the soul, the imagination, the inner world, not of travelling to a continent of vast open spaces, blue skies and rolling waves. Australia may be ripe for painters and photographers, but surely not for poets?

Dubai is ascending towards us and we have escaped the missiles. 'But what of that?'

The plane suddenly tilts: a line of skyscrapers appears giddily at the window, and yes, they're slantwise!

Dubai shimmers—
a runway stretching
the whole world over.

My sightseeing in Dubai consists of checking flight information.

I follow signs, go through security and stretch my legs along a corridor, past Arab men sailing along in voluminous white robes. Through vast polaroid windows I can see forty degrees of heat wobbling from the ground; skyscrapers and towers out of a futuristic Arabian Nights spike the horizon.

The departures lounge is filled with lugubrious be-suited

souls—oil executives, engineers, quantity surveyors—not a Bermuda shirt among us; we all behave as if we're in a doctor's waiting room, checking watches, letting out aggrieved sighs; and most of us are as still as corpses, with an obol under our tongues.

It is strange being in the Middle East—a place I've always dreamed about—but not in it at the same time. Airports are like the colonial outposts of a huge amorphous empire that has no capital city. The governors are the airport CEOs, the civil service are the air traffic controllers and the security officers the police force. Each colony has shops, a bank, a chapel, entertainments, places to stroll, cafés and cleaners, and the language spoken is a TEFL English reminiscent of 'Newspeak', in which the word 'great' becomes 'plusgood', and splendid becomes 'doubleplusgood'.

Every citizen seems to be affluent, and every citizen is homeless.

Seven hours down, seven more to Singapore.

> Flight information:
> Oslo, Tokyo, Moscow—where else
> will I never visit?

Time to Sin

Another plane, another take-off, another prayer to St Christopher.

This time I soar to the south of France via a film about Emile Zola and his friend Cézanne. The action is set in and around Zola's house in the country, surrounded by sun-dappled olive groves, hills and streams.

Zola is depicted as a bit of an Emily Dickinson, inhabiting an interior world, conducting his life from a quiet book-lined study, supremely comfortable in his quilted smoking jacket. Meanwhile the peppery Cézanne sets up his easel in various Arcadian glades and is driven to smash his canvases when his paintings fail to reach perfection. I remember his dictum: 'The day is coming when a single carrot, freshly observed, will set off a revolution.'

Later when I take the tin foil off the small container of my 'vegetarian option' an overcooked carrot winks at me.

Now we're travelling through the night and Chronos is performing a cunning sleight of hand.

> Time zones:
> Am I five hours younger?
> Or older?

The cramped seat, endless films and time-shift are working their subtle disorientation. I find a still point of the turning world in the kinetics of 'Flight Information' on my screen, updated by the minute. Facts and figures are as cosy as a hot water bottle. Miles travelled. Maps. More detailed maps. The ETA in Singapore is regularly flashed up under the heading 'Time to SIN', like a neon billboard in the garden of Eden.

My eyes are full of sleep but my mind is fighting it. Part of my fear of flying is common sense—along the lines of how the medieval pilgrim Felix Fabri felt about ships. Fabri recalled the ancient traveller Anacharsis saying that 'Those who are at sea cannot be counted among either the living or the dead because they are only removed from death by the space of four fingers, four fingers being the thickness of the sides of a ship'. Flying requires suppressing the imagination, something I am trained to do the exact opposite of.

Another reason for my aerophobia occurred after I saw a documentary about a rock star who had taken drugs during a flight and described how he had felt himself floating away from the plane into outer space, but at the same time being able to see his body on the plane. Hence my dread that if I go to sleep, my soul will drift off into the vast night and watch my body as it's left behind on the plane. Everything can be solved by simply not going to sleep.

It's nine o'clock in the morning. Time has done another long-jump and Singapore's skyline has sprung up from a sea of morning light, like a pop-up book of modernist architecture. Soon: Time to Sleep.

I have become an extra in *Zombie Apocalypse* making my way through customs, security and, finally, to the entrance area of the airport. Beyond the air-conditioned lobby the great steamy mass of Singapore city is waiting to embrace me.

> Baggage reclaim—
> end-of-term boarder,
> Mum last to arrive.

About the only thing I know about Singapore is Raffles Hotel, and the Second World War, when the British general Arthur Percival handed over the city to the Japanese, the largest surrender of British-led military personnel in history. I recall that in 1920 the brutally efficient Percival had been a young intelligence officer in the Essex

Regiment in Ireland during the War of Independence. The regiment was stationed in West Cork to root out the IRA and had even used my tiny village as a local operational centre, requisitioning the local Catholic primary school as an HQ. The very same school which was later turned into a house, and where I now live. Percival might have slept in my bedroom.

And I remember a village neighbour describing how her father had been one of many local men rounded up by the Essex soldiers and forced-marched to an internment camp. When her father became elderly, about the only thing he could remember was tramping down a local lane, hands on his head, and a British soldier saying to him incessantly in a whining voice, 'Give us a fag, Paddy. Give us a fag, Paddy'.

A taxi to my hotel would be quicker; but there is so much current news about Islamic State at the moment and hostages and kidnapping that my brain, gnawing news like a rodent, keeps popping in the idea that the driver is a fanatic and next thing I'll be chained to a radiator. I opt for the hotel's tiny shuttle bus—at least I will have the silent intimacy of complete strangers.

The vehicle is a ten-seater and the driver is curt. When we're all crammed in, he lets out a heavy Sisyphean sigh, turns over the diesel engine into deep-throated chicken clucking and continues his day of eternal circuits.

'The Mystic East'

I try to feel excited. For the first time ever I'm in—clash of gong—the *mystic east*. The road to Mandalay, pagodas! But so far everything is *uber*-occidental. Limousines, skyscrapers, suits, ties, summer dresses; it's like entering the humidity of a vast cosmic greenhouse and finding yourself in Frankfurt. I feel less intrigued, somehow, than when I was on holiday in County Laois as a child and saw an Otherworld of hedgerows, low hills, Norman ruins and drizzle on the whitethorns. Perhaps it's all to do with your age when you see something.

> The airport road unzipping
> the tin light of Singapore—
> dis-orienting.

We head for the centre and eventually chug past Raffles Hotel, an over-iced wedding-cake hemmed in by frantic roads. I'd been fantasising about having a Singapore Sling in the bar at Raffles, as one does, but someone told me the hotel had been bought by a new owner, who was reserving the bar area for residents only.

> Raffles:
> riff-raff-
> less.

As we motor along I keep thinking that at any moment Singapore must at some point burst into *oriental* scenes, like the start of a James

Bond film—that we'll turn a corner and get hopelessly mired in street markets, rickshaws, chickens in cages, peasants wearing loose cotton clothes and sandals. My kingdom for a stereotype! Alack, the conditioned mind!

We head out west to my hotel, which turns out to be yet another rendering of muzak in vertical concrete.

The receptionist is a charming but over-fawning Indian lad, who keeps complimenting me on my hat, which is broad-brimmed and made of grey-green fabric. I had bought it, second-hand, in order to blend in with Australians. What he doesn't know is that ever since I got it I've been worried it will make me look foolish. It unnerves me when he keeps saying with a big smile: 'That's a fine hat you have there, sir. It's certainly a super-cool hat, sir. Oh, yes, super-cool.'

I crash out on my bed, my body still maintaining its foetal aircraft-seat position, but now at least set horizontally.

> After the flight
> drifting into sleep—
> the hotel taking off.

I wake up. Day-glow hands of my clock tell me it's 4 pm, but my body is adrift somewhere on the sea of midnight.

I venture out onto the streets of Singapore and realise what a clever trick the air-conditioning has been playing: it's more than thirty degrees and low grey clouds have sealed in the humidity. It's like swimming in warm asthma.

The famous but cruelly named Orchard Road is flanked by giant hedgerows … of modernist department stores selling delectable fruits of perfumes, shoes and handbags. The road is more of an inner-city highway, up to six lanes across, and stretches as far as the eye can see; huge crowds gather by traffic lights; the gents in jackets, the ladies in shorts, and almost everyone seems to be wearing glasses. A large young man waddles across the road and is so slowed up by his need to text while he walks that I fret the straining traffic lights will unleash a stampede of cars on him.

Out of the blue I feel giddy; perhaps the heat, density of buildings and people; perhaps the flights, the distance travelled, lack of sleep and change of time zones. I remember Sir Laurens van der Post citing the Kalahari Bushmen's notion that on long journeys the body has to pause to allow the soul to catch up.

I sit down on a bench and take a few polluted breaths, but my soul feels a long way away, as if it's still lingering in Clonakilty. Here I am, a dot among five million people on a small island—equivalent to the population of Ireland being transported to the Isle of Man. I don't know a single person in the place; more to the point, there's nothing to make me feel at home spiritually, no crumbly old castle or ancient cemetery or medieval church. No building seems older than twenty years.

Because Singapore's population is a mishmash of Malays, Chinese, Thai and Indians, who all communicate with each other in English, there's a post-Babel atmosphere of people trying to find a common tongue. All the outward trappings of a Western city are present and correct, but bigger and more gleaming, while the roads and pavements are spookily tidy.

I continue my dopey peregrinations, and my spirits lift feebly when I see tree-lined side-streets with lovely old names: Dublin Road, Exeter Road. I choose Killiney Road—named after a leafy district of south Dublin—which has a line of low-key restaurants with outdoor tables under awnings.

I walk up and down, not daring to take the plunge. I'm easily put off by groups of locals tucking into rice and noodles, feeling that if I walked in they would all look round as one and stare at me, noodles dripping from half-open mouths like walrus tusks. But I'm also put off by the emptier establishments, with sleepy, hangdog fellas behind the counter. There's a Chinese café with a neon-lit menu advertising 'Claypot porridge with frogs legs'. This is accompanied by a helpful image showing a bowl of grey mess with little green legs sticking out of it. Next door is a Thai café with tinkling music; then another

Chinese restaurant, which calls itself 'Jew Kit' for some reason—perhaps meaning it serves kosher Jewish food (Kit = Kitchen?). It refers to its 'Operating Hours'—perhaps it's a surgery in disguise, a vet amputating frogs for porridge?

Going for the Thai café, I sit at a pavement table by myself. I do my checks: enough Singapore dollars; no hidden charges on the menu; vegetarian food. A waiter comes and I can't believe how smooth the process is. He speaks perfect English and has a friendly manner. I sit back and, for the first time in what seems an eternity, almost relax, or, more precisely, I don't quite not relax. I feel pretty proud. Here I am in Singapore by myself, ordering food in a café. Surely this makes me—the person who gets anxious trying to find a parking spot in Clonakilty—a fully-fledged international traveller. Even the disjointed music is sounding pleasant and vaguely familiar. The notes begin to hit memory cells and yes, it's an infinitely tinkly baroque version of 'Bridge Over Troubled Water'.

As my food arrives the melody changes to 'Auld Lang Syne', a festive accompaniment to my mixed veg rice, two bottles of water, and mango and sticky rice for pudding. For my in-house meal entertainment—a habit I have acquired from watching aeroplane screens for fourteen hours—I gaze at the building opposite. It's the underground car park of Singapore Telecom. It seems pleasantly familiar and stable and reassuring. Then I notice that as each car arrives, two thin white-haired men dressed in grey emerge from the shadows like ghosts, wielding bomb detectors on the end of long metal rods. They sweep the bottoms of the cars for devices in a routine that has the compulsion of Russian roulette.

> Glitter of Orchard Road:
> the night is missing
> the Milky Way.

Next morning. I pull the curtain and my vision is flooded by the grey bulk of the neighbouring hotel—I hadn't realised it was only a handful of yards away; my window is like a sad square eye, long accustomed to the prospect of a creeping cataract.

My flight to Melbourne is in the evening, and therefore there's time to kill—if only I could hunt down the scattered hours first. I decamp to the hotel's small swimming pool, which lies like a royal blue button below a tall grey suit. Even out of the sun it's too hot and dazzling to read. I lie on a lounger and bake in the oven of the shade.

Later, I retrieve my bags and hat from reception. The young Indian is there: 'We have taken good care of your hat, sir, your cool hat.' Still no irony, but he makes me anxious. Will I dare wear it in Australia? I need a hat. My hair is too thin, my skin too fair.

The taxi to the airport is courtesy of a driver who has one arm in a sling and seems to have developed in his other one compensatory joints and muscles to weave in and out of traffic lanes. Meanwhile, he rattles off Singaporean history and his experiences in Melbourne. 'You must go Victoria Market—so cute! You see central reservation in this road? Look solid, right? with all the flower beds. But God, man, it's moveable. Why? Because the Air Force can roll it up and use road for an airstrip. See that sports stadium—retractable roof. One Direction play there, last year was it? God, man, my daughter says they're one cute band.' He drops me off and I shake his one good hand and give him one cute tip.

> Singapore
> taximan:
>   one arm
> two eyes
>   for all—
> except
>   the swerving road.

At the airport I potter, muddle, fuss, sit for a while. I check, re-check my watch and saunter to the departures lounge, daydreaming.

Australia now seems disturbingly less unreal. In seven hours I will be looking down on the coastline I used to draw at primary school with the aid of a plastic template. I never really understood why lesson after lesson we had to study savannah grassland and merino sheep. Australia—the place we'd dig to on beach holidays; the land of Christmas turkey on the beach, barbies in the backyard, the land of the long white socks, streets thronging with tall smiley women and bronzed footy jocks wearing vests and swathes of tattoos. But also the land of my putative ancestor, Charles Harpur, known as the 'father of Australian poetry', and one of the first native-born white Australian poets. It's my hope I'll be able to get onto the Charles Harpur trail at some point.

> Australia everywhere—
> a croissant, a slice of soda bread
> after a Bight.

The departures lounge is unexpectedly empty. I must be far too early.

There's a thoughtfully placed water dispenser—I start filling my bottle while humming 'Waltzing Matilda' to myself when I hear a shout from the door: 'Hurry up sir, you're the last one on the plane!'

I look over my shoulder and can't see whom the official is talking to. I keep filling my bottle.

'You must go NOW, sir, the plane is ready for take-off!'

Still filling my bottle and humming I turn round and see him glaring at me, then I look at my watch. I never changed the flipping time! I am an hour behind. I shoot across the lounge and into a tunnel that's like a birth canal projecting me towards the door of the plane.

I plunge like some scrappy newborn thing into a blurry sea of wedged-in weary faces and feel a volley of a thousand eyes shooting me down. I mumble apologies to a Qantas flight attendant and her male colleague, both refreshingly in their fifties, with lived-in faces and a bit overweight and cheery, like an uncle and aunt. For my pains I receive my first indigenous 'No worries, sir', spoken with such genuine warmth I want them to adopt me as their son.

The flight takes place at night, but again we will do a sudden kangaroo jump into the morning.

The aircraft lights are dimmed and inklings of sleepiness insinuate themselves. I almost succumb, but jolt myself awake before my soul floats off—by recalling there are less than four inches of aircraft between me and oblivion.

I watch a film about Abraham Lincoln but cannot concentrate: what will Australia hold? I'll be house-sitting in Fitzroy, the arty quarter of Melbourne, in a place owned by two retired teachers, Yolande and David, whom I've never met before, themselves off to New York for three weeks. My one big duty is to look after their ancient cat, Sappho. Will she mew at me in dithyrambs? Can I remember enough ancient Greek to respond in kind?

I picture a small house, a sunny backyard and a few weeks of writing and revising poems. I want to see a bit of the outback and Australian art; meet a poet or two. See a wallaby. And then a week in Sydney with an old university friend. 'Time to MEL' keeps being updated. Time to mellow, please God, time to mellow …

G'day

We touch down at 6 am in Melbourne. Australia! Australia, *mate*.

I feel I ought to kiss the runway or break open a beer or sing the out-of-tune version of 'Advance Australia Fair' as patented by the Australian rugby team.

The airport lobby is relatively small and homely. A young woman with pigtails that have a springy life of their own is driving a baggage buggy, and smiles and giggles as she weaves in and out of flat-footed travellers in a new game she's just invented for herself. Already I feel sunny, carefree, lucky.

Outside the terminal there's a vast pink sky stretched across a long flat horizon. I've shrunk in size, like Alice, and I'm standing upright on the bottom of the Antipathies.

> The space of Australia
> o p e n s
> t h e s o u l

I am soon brought down to earth by my Greek taxi driver, who tells me his life story in broken English. And not just that. He insists on telling me the foibles of taxi drivers of different nationalities, and none too complimentary. I'm too excited-exhausted-sleepy to take much in.

I arrive in Fitzroy with its streets of single-storeyed Victorian terraced houses, which look small and neat on the outside but, as I will find out, stretch backwards into substantial dwellings. Bushy trees and creepers spill over the picket fence of 'my' house, shielding most of it from the quiet road. I should be nervous, but I'm too jet-lagged. I knock and David answers, as shinily bald as me but slightly taller, smiley, glasses, wearing shorts; then Yolande pops up, slender, dark-haired, short pony tail, Mediterranean-looking. Both of them welcoming and humorous.

We sit and have coffee. Yolande, it turns out, is interested in ancient Greece and archaeology, while David in history and English literature. Everything, mirabile dictu, that I like. Their living room is soulful with its wood panelling and shelves of books that I have either read or, mainly, would want to read; the whole canon of Western culture, in fact. As we are chatting away, I hear a plaintive meow and there is Sappho! my new housemate, creaking towards me. I give her a stroke and a pat, the first of many in the next few weeks, and make endearing noises. She looks at me as if she's thinking, 'Cut the crap'. Already I suppose it will be a wrench to leave her at the end of my stay.

I don't consider myself a natural cat person. I always thought of them as being too groomed, sly, murderous, self-interested … until I met Eileen's cat Toots. A delicate tortoiseshell, Toots had wandered into Eileen's life when she was living in her first flat in Acton, London, in a ramshackle extension to a crumbly old church. At first I ignored Toots as best I could, but before long I was hooked. The beauty, the capriciousness, the adorable idiosyncrasies. When Eileen decided to return to Australia in the mid-1990s I was heartbroken. I knew I would be in contact with Eileen, but the spectre of her taking Toots off to a new owner was too much. To think of strangers stroking her, feeding her, dangling her toy mouse … In a fit of commemoration I wrote my first cat poem, written after the style of 'My Cat Jeoffrey' by the eighteenth-century English poet Christopher Smart. Perhaps I'll be composing another poem in honour of Sappho?

Eileen's Cat Toots
(After Christopher Smart)

I will praise Eileen's cat Toots
For she is chieftain of the pussy race
For she wears her tartan ribbon round her neck
For she bears the markings of a tortoise
For her snowy feet are soft as thistledown
For her cheeks are plump like pin-cushions
For her tail is a feather boa
For she concertinas out to be a draught excluder by the door
For she lies like the sphinx and folds her mitts into her winter muffler
For her back leg is like a rabbit's and as biteable
For when she sees the movement of a sparrow she twitches forward,
    red alert
For she is a wicked puss, an eater of God's creatures,
For she is a blesséd puss, and knows not what she doeth
For when she leaps she stretches like a caterpillar and alights
    as softly as a butterfly
For she tiptoes like a ballerina through the table's bric-a-brac
For she gets her artificial tan beneath the angle-poise
For her eyes are moss-green marbles of light
For her wee head fills her bowl of food when she crunches up her
    fish-meal beans
For she eats her blobs of porridge from your finger
For she is a waif with a look of desolation when she cries out for more
    food
For her tongue laps the vase's water like a tiny darting goldfish
For her teeth are sleek and creamy like bone needles
For she biffs her mouse of silver foil and lays in ambush below
    the table
For she can't resist an interest in the drumming of the fingers
For on bonfire night she creeps two millimetres from the floor

For when it thunders she seeks out an air-raid shelter in the
    washing basket
For when she arches up her back she is a Chinese bridge
For she looks so innocent when told she'd make a nice fur hat
For she settles on the window sill to greet you home from work
For she steams in from the cat flap: entry pursued by a Tom
For at night she is a furry-covered water-bottle at your feet
For when she wakes she lifts a sultry peeper and yawns out
    her claws
For she sits in backyard sunlight and lifts a drumstick leg to lick
    her fur
For she's a tiger in her jungle of lupins and gladioli
For she is a wee angel, Agnus Dei, and brings light to people's eyes
For she makes me think of Eileen, wherever she may roam, on
    this side, or on that side, of the world

As I go off for a jet-lag siesta, David warns me I might be woken by
a possum crashing down on the roof. I realise I have no idea what a
possum is. Is it something like a raccoon? Mind you, I'm not even
sure what a raccoon is—something like a lemur? As if I knew what
a lemur was … David also says that the newspaper boy tends to hurl
the rolled-up newspaper at the bedroom window early in the morn-
ing. Perhaps he'll scare off the kamikaze possum.

I emerge blinkingly in the early evening and am led like Samson to
the temple of a tapas bar up the main road. Fitzroy on first blurry
inspection is bohemian and chic, every shop a vegetarian café, or
Vietnamese bistro, or craft beer shop, and the pavements full of tanned
good-looking carefree youths; everyone seems to be on holiday.
    The tapas bar is called 'Naked for Satan'. Time to Mel and Time to
Sin? The name in fact derives from a time when the building in its
early history was a gin distillery and workers in the basement had
to strip off because of the heat. Thus it was said they were 'naked for
Satan'.

Fully buttoned-up for Satan, I climb many flights of stairs to the rooftop, not without trepidation: I haven't let on, yet, that I'm scared of heights. I'm conscious that for the first time ever, I'm with two real, live Australians in Australia, and I don't want to appear to be more wimpish than they must think I am already—from insistent questions about how to work the washing machine and reaction to the possum jumping on the roof.

The rooftop is teeming with young people, as if every nearby office is holding a party here—'the young in one another's arms …' as Yeats once wrote … 'no country for old men'. Crucially it's not too vertiginous, and I can stomach the views reaching across the city. I can see 'iconic' Melbourne buildings to the south, mostly skyscrapers, less obtrusive than Singapore's; to the east the sprawling campus of the university lies under a pure blue sky. David strikes a sour note by mentioning in a sinisterly casual way the presence of fruit bats, 'quite large actually'. How is it that 'quite' always means the extreme opposite?

We find a table and drink beer. I risk having it in a glass and not swigging it from a bottle like the twenty-somethings. I hear a voice say, 'Nah, nah, nah, only sheilas drink from glasses, mate … but it's only my own.

We are soon joined by Kevin, a poet whom I met in West Cork for a day when he was visiting Ireland. He is also a professor of creative writing, and it was he who put me in touch with David and Yolande, old friends of his. He is a benign, wiry man about my age, with a beard, glasses, and well-grooved laughter lines. His good crop of hair is also wiry, brown with a scattering of grey. He is quietly spoken and seems to have fifty different intonations for the word 'yeah' that express all sorts of subtleties, ranging from direct affirmations to gentle scepticism. 'Yeah.' 'Oh-Yeh.' 'Yeaah?' 'Yé-ah!'

I talk to David about politics and ask him what the correct name is for the country's indigenous population. I explain that when I wrote an article about Uluru in the 1980s, I was told by the Australian Embassy to refer to them as Aborigines. He shakes his head. 'Nah,

nah. That's not it now. Maybe Aboriginal peoples, Indigenous Australians—those two are probably the best of the bunch.' Then he pauses and thinks for a while and I wait for the big revelation: 'Listen, whatever phrase you use, you won't be right.'

By the time we leave the boozy bosom of Satan, the sky has turned a deep, dark blue. The air is still warm and Melbourne has become a panorama of fairy lights. I can barely remember Singapore, let alone West Cork.

We stroll home through side streets, passing en route an Irish bar where Kevin and I will do a reading later on in the month.

Back home, David and Yolande, who have to leave early in the morning for New York, give me final instructions and advice before taking to their beds. I hardly get my trousers off before I'm aslee …

> First nighter in Oz—
> beneath the eiderdown
> down under in the land of Nod.

Follow the moon

Friday. By the time I wake up, wondering what bed, what room, house, city, country, continent I'm in, David and Yolande are already at the airport, waiting to swap countries. I realise it is 17 March and think of the St Patrick's Day parade soon to take place back home in my little town of Clonakilty. The narrow main street will be lined with mums and dads wearing green leprechaun top hats and waving flags, cheering on the schools' parades and various floats. I chuckle at the memory of last year's parade when one of the 'floats' consisted of a single undecorated, unfestooned tractor driven by a farmer who had taken the opportunity to stick a 'For Sale' sign on his machine.

> St Patrick's Day
> in … Melbourne?
> Snakes alive!

I feel spacey. I'm all alone on this vast continent. Priorities. Toast, teeth, then … look out Australia!

> Straps loosened
> my suitcase world
> fills the universe.

First of all I need to scavenge for food like a demented dingo. Rucksack on back, sun cream plastered on, I walk a few hundred yards to my nearest supermarket, Coles, and hope my credit card won't be annulled by an overzealous bank clerk back home, spotting purchases from Melbourne. I did warn them before leaving, but … I notice most of the check-outs are dreaded self-service and I don't fancy calling for inevitable assistance. The pinging of barcodes sounds like an ancient computer game that I don't want to play.

Luckily there's one check-out that is, luxury of luxuries, manned by a human being.

The shoppers look familiar but somehow different; there's a retro feel to everyone; youths with punk hairdos and nose rings; a man with a biker's long shaggy hair but wearing a tie and sober grey suit.

When I reach the check-out I take out my credit card and feel nervous out of all proportion to the transaction. I smile apologetically, as if I know I'm going to fail a lie-detector. But the card sails through with flying colours and I lug a rucksack and three plastic bags full of a week's food back home through twenty-seven degrees of heat.

> Angry with autumn,
> Melbourne in March
> rages like July.

In the evening I am off to supper at Kevin's house in Brunswick a few miles away to meet his son and daughter—his wife is currently working in the outback—and a poet friend of his called Grant. He said he'd meet me on his bike near the university, put me on a tram then pick me up at the appropriate stop and lead us home. He made it sound so easy—all I have to do is walk along the road by the old cemetery and he will spot me.

Nothing is easy with jet lag. I feel as if I might stack the beers in the oven.

I set out with a map, negotiate dual carriageways and sure enough, there's the municipal cemetery, where I'm surprised to see a group of Jewish gravestones inscribed with Hebrew words and stars of David and menorahs. The rush-hour traffic is pouring past me and I'm feeling like a needle in a haystack, when Kevin arrives out of nowhere, his head enshelled with a helmet, his body organically attached to his bike, like a giant mutant beetle. He dismounts and leads me to the nearest tram stop, talking me through the straightforward tram procedure. Of course it's not quite straightforward—the tram travels in the middle of the hectic highway and it looks as if you have to cross a stream of aggressive traffic to get to it, until you know that cars aren't allowed to pass on the tram's inside. You then have to swipe your 'Myki' card when you get on, but it isn't clear whether you swipe it to get off; it all depends if you're in a 'free zone' or not. Or maybe it doesn't matter. Kevin's not sure, but gives me his best advice: 'Watch the others,' he says cheerfully. 'I'll bike off and meet you four stops down.'

The tram duly arrives and I get on and swipe, then scrutinise every departing passenger, like a geek who's swapped train-spotting for Myki-card-spotting. I look so shifty. I weigh up the evidence and conclude I won't have to swipe to get off.

I meet Kevin at the designated stop and we walk along broad quietening roads to a part of Brunswick that looks far more twentieth century than Fitzroy; the houses have open front gardens and are less shoe-horned into the streets. Kevin owns a stylish detached house that stands out among a row of artisan cottages. Inside I am greeted by his daughter, Sophie, a law student, and ushered into a living room-cum-kitchen with big windows looking out onto a neat back garden. Sophie is angelically making supper for us.

> Giant pizzas:
> so round, so smiley—
> these Neapolitan faces!

I am sent out to the backyard to pick fruits from a beautiful fig tree. Feeling like Adam daydreaming about the nature of good and evil, I hear a sound I've never heard before—so sudden and loud and with such a pulse I think it must be a car alarm; it turns out to be a chorus of crickets.

Interrupting the crickets' call to vespers, a loud knock on the door announces the arrival of Kevin's friend Grant and his Chinese partner Tang Yi and her mother, who, it turns out, has as much English as I have Mandarin. Grant is a wry, humorous soul and straightaway thrusts a book of his poems into my hands by way of an introduction. We soon discover we are fans of Bashō as well as the Indian-born spiritual thinker Jiddu Krishnamurti, a rare event in any part of the world.

We are soon joined by a young Danish lad, a friend of Kevin's son. He is tall, well-built from labouring on building sites, blond and cheerful—just how I imagined Australian men, in fact—and we get into talking about our dream jobs. I try to guess his. Sports psychologist? Rock guitarist? No. It turns out that he wants to design and build skateboarding parks in Nepal. And there I was imagining Nepalese kids would be thumbing through Sanskrit literature or training to be sherpas, not hurtling towards 'vert' walls, banks, pyramids, quarter pipes and kink rails.

We make a motley but genial crew, and the evening goes well, though I do have occasional flashes of geographical vastness and cosmic disorientation. What would Krishnamurti say? 'You take your home with you; home is a state of being at one with yourself—when there is no separation between you, the observer, and what you observe. A big house, slum house, foreign country at the bottom of the world, it doesn't matter.' Something like that.

Filled with pizza and good cheer, I decide to quit while I'm winning and head back to Fitzroy; Grant gamely volunteers to drive me home. Approaching my house, we lose our way in a maze of small residential one-way streets; we pause by a house from which a group of partygoers has spilled out into the warm night. I wind down my window and Grant shouts across to the nearest person, a mature glamorous woman, a bit tipsy, who straightaway berates him angrily for not having SatNav—she seems scarily incensed until with a big smile she invites us all to her party. It's so very tempting, but we decline graciously and she gives Grant eccentric directions.

Back home, Sappho greets me, meowing for food and wanting to party.

Lost in Fitzroy:
'Follow the moon'—
she points at the night
with a globe of white wine.

Close to Homer

I wake up and check the time and the date: Saturday 18 March. That means that back in Cork it's still Friday and St Paddy's Day. I still feel the need to anchor myself in an old ticking grandfather clock and translate antipodean time into Irish time, but I imagine that will pass.

I feed Sappho, lobbing a gobbet of pre-prepared frozen meat onto the backyard. She loses her arthritis for a moment and fills the space over the meat with her little furry head. I suddenly remember that Kevin is coming round to pick me up to go to a friend of his, an elderly, blind literary editor named John. Kevin was due to visit and read poetry to him today and suggested I came along too.

Kevin arrives on his bike and we take a tram to Brunswick.

John has a modern flat, all kitted out to compensate for his lack of sight. He is a thin, wiry, white-haired man, graceful, learned and has a black patch on one side of his glasses, which gives him the air of a genteel pirate enjoying his retirement from the Seven Seas. He likes having poems read to him and insists on me reading a few of my own. I tell him about my interest in Charles Harpur—whose work John knows and likes. I tell him that Charles's father, Joseph, was a Protestant Harpur from Kinsale in Cork, and that there are so few Protestant Harpurs with a 'u' spelling in Ireland that I think it highly probable there's some link with my own family.

I talk about Charles's interest, like mine, in things spiritual but also his rejecting institutionalised religion; his interest, like mine, in Homer; and his struggle to write poetry while trying to earn a living at jobs that didn't suit him. During the last bleak period of his life, when he had TB, he was copying into his notebook his translation of four lines of Homer. I read the lines out to John and Kevin from the copy of Charles's *Selected* I've brought with me:

> The race of men is as the race of leaves:
> Some the winds shed upon the ground, while still
> The fructifying boughs put others forth,
> To flourish in their season. So of men
> The generations die and are renewed.

I tell John and Kevin about the frisson I'd had when I discovered those lines—because they were exactly the same four lines I myself had recently translated for an Irish radio broadcast.

> Our lives are like the cycle of leaves.
> The wind scatters the old leaves across the earth,
> then spring returns and trees put forth new growth.
> That's how it is with human beings:
> the generations come and go, go and come.

I could picture Charles staring at those Greek lines, mindful of the great operations of the universe, and trying to find the right English words and rhythm for them, just as I had tried to do 150 years later.

Charles died in 1868, shortly after writing out 'The race of men …' Judging by his self-written obituary, his state of mind was precarious. I read out this obituary to John and Kevin, which begins: 'Here lies Charles Harpur, who at fifty years of age came to the conclusion, that he was living in a sham age, under a sham Government, and amongst sham friends, and that any World whatever must therefore be a better world than theirs …' The obituary goes on in this vein and I find it difficult reading it to the end.

Kevin and I leave John and walk back to Kevin's home in Brunswick. Outside in his backyard there is a surprise visitor in the shape of a baby possum tucked into the side of a wall, so curled up you can't tell its head from its tail. It's just a circular shape, a furry ammonite. Kevin wonders whether it is sick, or whether his cat has traumatised or wounded it. He then drives me home.

> Blind writer's books—
> spines gathering memories
> gathering dust.

Possum

Something wakes me up late morning on Sunday, 19 March and I know it's not my alarm clock: it sounds like a distant telephone ringing, but then I track it down to Sappho's plaintive morning meow, which is identical to her plaintive evening meow. I get up and go to the fridge to get her meat ration. I suspect she would flounce at me if she weren't so arthritic.

I've had only two full days in Australia and it feels like a month. The autumn morning is already hot and heavy; the backyard is filled with lush plants and a big shady tree where a large possum is supposedly lurking. I check my scribbled notes and see that Kevin is coming round. He'd told me he was meeting an old poet friend of his from Tasmania and said I could come along too if I wished. I did wish, and suggested they both come to Fitzroy for lunch. I'm not a cook, but I can shop at Coles and chop and heat up as well as anyone.

Kevin arrives slightly early. He is looking sad. I wonder whether it's about his mother, a nonagenarian who is in hospital struggling to recover from a fall.

'You know that baby possum in the backyard? It died. We buried it this morning.'

We fall into a silence and I can sense we both feel like shedding a tear. That poor little bundle of dark fur. Any death connects you to other deaths. The suddenness, the abrupt termination of warm life. Perhaps Kevin is also thinking of his mum? I can't help thinking of Philip Larkin's poem, 'The Mower', in which he accidentally kills a hedgehog while mowing the grass. A hedgehog he'd personally fed with milk. The poem ends with the sentiment: 'The first day after a death, the new absence / Is always the same; we should be careful / Of each other, we should be kind / While there is still time.' It turned out that Larkin's own mother had died not long before the death of the hedgehog.

A cheery shout at the open front door changes our mood. Lyndon of Tasmania is here. He looks as if he's in his early sixties, blondish, perspiring, soft-voiced, open and frank, pleased to see Kevin again. He used to be in a successful rock band and is now a psychotherapist down in Tasmania. I let them catch up on news and lay out Coles's best fare: a quiche, tomatoes, wine and strawberry mousse tartlets.

At lunch the main topic of conversation is a book of poems Kevin has edited. Lyndon is particularly interested in the book because it has been written by his ex-partner, a woman who in various poems refers to Lyndon as being a bit of a bastard, or worse. I question Lyndon about this—surely, this is going to be embarrassing, humiliating, damaging? But it turns out to be a case of 'no worries'. She is entitled to her opinion, he says, and he admires her honesty.

They leave mid-afternoon. I wash up and flop on the sofa. I have to revise my notes for a long-prearranged visit to a school in the country tomorrow, but it's too hot to think. Sappho grinds towards me, meowing steadily like a distant ambulance siren. She manages to clamber up onto the sofa and, despite my protests—the sofa is technically off-limits to her—she bats away my resistance and finds a spot that suits her on my lap.

> Backyard baby possum
> asleep in a ball;
> still a day from death.

School

I jolt awake from a huge crash overhead—something has smashed into the roof and for a moment I can't think what it is—it's as if a paratrooper has jumped onto it with heavy combat boots. Am I hostage? Am I chained to a radiator? Then I remember it must be the possum. I had no idea possums could sound so big.

My head is buzzing with blurry details. Monday? Yes! Monday. School day. The school in the country, just beyond Melbourne. When I mailed Claire, the school's English teacher, to ask how to get there, she wrote: 'Very easy—download a tram app onto your iPhone and hop on a tram into the city centre (you'll need to buy a Myki card—sold at lots of milk bars etc.). You'll probably come down Swanston Street from wherever you are in Fitzroy—so you get off that tram at Bourke Street and hop on another one (free tram) to Southern Cross station.'

Tram app? iPhone? Two types of tram? Lots of worries, mate.

I spend the day re-checking things to bring. It's an overnight stay. I need notes for the talk I have to give in the evening. And notes for the two classes I have to preside at next day. Toothbrush. Water. Feed Sappho and top up her food.

Just getting to Southern Cross will feel like a major achievement.

I plaster suncream on my face then check in the mirror that I don't have what my friend Ian calls my 'failed geisha girl' look. I definitely do not look 'failed'.

*

I catch a tram, wield my Myki as masterfully as Excalibur, and sail down into central Melbourne for the first time. Huge skyscrapers, trees erupting from pavements and old columned colonial buildings line the streets, with trams crisscrossing my sightline all the time.

At Southern Cross station I board the train and try to study the other passengers surreptitiously. Australians are still exotic creatures, and it's a fascinating game trying to guess their professions and ethnic backgrounds. Almost all of them have their heads down, transfixed by screens.

I look at my notes and keep replaying in my head what my old school friend Jonesy said on the phone when I told him about the school visit and my speculations as to how they would introduce me at the talk. Jonesy gave it a second's thought then said in a broad Australian accent, with a climactic intonation: 'Well, what have we here!?' It summed up all my fears in five words.

I get out at a tiny station in the middle of nowhere; the platform is a skinny island bordered on either side by single-track rails. I feel like Spencer Tracey in *Bad Day at Black Rock*. I am to be met by Claire, who is actually English. I have no idea what she looks like, but at least I'll know her from her accent.

I wait for a while, gazing across the tracks at a soulless car park and a shopping mall with boarded-up shop windows. Eventually two figures arrive, a burly man with big black-framed glasses and a woman in jeans, a fringe, blue eyes.

'Are you James?'

The woman's accent is so Australian that I can't believe it's the Claire I have been mailing for weeks. I had imagined a Victorian governess with a floral summer dress, a wide-brimmed hat and a parasol. Her colleague, Lloyd, is hearty, and both of them are in high spirits, like kids playing truant.

*

We arrive at school, which looks like a huge university campus—little driveways around pools of manicured lawns and red-brick buildings, a science block, a 'health and wellbeing' block (i.e. sports hall), various boarding houses, and a large sweep of playing fields that go down to the sea. Although the campus looks civilised and benign, it triggers memories of my own teenage boarding experience. My own school was a maze of corridors intersecting within a huge red-brick Victorian shell, and I remember in my first week getting lost on the way to a lesson in some distant corner of the main building—and becoming totally disorientated, feeling a mixture of sea- and home-sickness. I recorded the experience in a verse memoir about being a boarder; this sequence of poems was responsible, as winner of the Vincent Buckley Prize, for bringing me to this school:

The Perfect Tense

The bell a sizzling ECT stops dead.
Classroom doors slam shut, the train
is ready to leave and I'm marooned
in creeping quiet as if I'm going deaf
or the school's playing out a game
of sardines and I'm the last one left.

I skelter down the endless platform
but only find a deeper absence
and all I see are two contrasting doors:

one opens to a room, the glare of classmates,
a master pausing from the perfect tense;

the other to a world beyond the gates
the village road with puddles full of sky.

an Austin like my mother's passing by.

Claire and Lloyd are oblivious of my throwback to boarding school heebie-jeebies and whisk me around the chapel, war memorial, dining hall and the lecture theatre, where I shall later give my talk. Lloyd shows me where I will stand, and where he will introduce me. I think of Jonesy's predicted intro and try not smirk, especially when Lloyd says: 'So, you'll be parked there, by the lectern, and I'll come up and I'll say something like … Heeerrre's James!' I suddenly think Jonesy might be horribly psychic. Whatever introduction Lloyd gives, I will struggle not to giggle.

We adjourn to a private dining room for supper with the English faculty staff—mostly women, middle-aged, jolly, open, sociable. Also present is a retired master called Strazz, short of stature, sartorial, grey-crinkly-haired in a distinguished way, wearing a pale jacket and tie, and who, it turns out, is writing a biography of Vincent Buckley, the poet who has caused me to be here. The teachers are in great form, not least because of the wine and porcini mushrooms and tomato pasta. I make chit-chat and smother my nerves with mouthfuls of cheesecake and blueberry compote.

Afterwards I am led to the lecture hall; a small firing squad of an audience drifts in, mostly English teachers with a few pupils and a parent or two. When Lloyd introduces me I'm almost disappointed it's not: 'Well, what have we here?!' It's much more formal and dignified; I feel no temptation to giggle. Lloyd sits down and Claire comes up to say a few words about me. I remember my daughter Arin's public speaking advice: 'Dad, when you give your talk, make sure your first line hooks them and make sure your flies are done up.'

Claire announces she is going to read one of my poems, and it turns out it's the one I was intending to end my talk with. The poem commemorates my first girlfriend Sarah's father, Professor Gordon Hamilton-Fairley, a cancer specialist who was killed by an IRA bomb in London in 1975. He was taking his two dogs for a walk outside his London home and one of them triggered a car bomb intended for his politician neighbour. Gordon had been born in Australia and educated at this very school before migrating to England, and it seemed fitting to read the poem to end the talk. Claire and I do a hurried negotiation and we decide it's best if she reads the poem first.

After her recital of the poem, I launch into my talk, moving from Horace to Homer to Charles Harpur. I cannot gauge how the audience is taking it. Too low-brow, high-brow, middle-brow, furrowed-brow? God knows. Afterwards, Strazz the Sartorial is, sweetly, in a flutter about it: 'Ah, a long while since I've heard lines of Horace spoken here …'

It's been a long day. Claire drives me back to her house—the 'seaside shack' as she has described it—which lies beside Bells Beach, one of the top surfing spots in the world.

Night has descended and the shack reveals itself to be a huge rambling ranch with paddocks and a long drive, which she uses as both a home and a B and B.

I'm virtually teetotal, but we have two bottles of wine and exchange life stories. How she morphed from an upper-middle-class English rose into an Aussie sheep farmer's wife in the middle of the outback is a transformation to impress even Ovid. I have nothing to match that, my life being measured out in books, and rooms in which to read them.

> Bells Beach
> night air
> sea-dark wine …

Riddles

Tuesday morning. For my benefit Claire puts out birdseed in the courtyard to attract the galahs, and like harpies they duly swoop down—a bustle of parrots with pink bodies and frothy white heads, like raspberry milkshakes on wings. My first taste of exotic Australian birdlife.

We hop into Claire's car—but not before I spy a small kangaroo (my first one!) in the paddocks. It feels like a seminal moment, like seeing a shamrock in Ireland or a Beefeater in London. The roo spots me and freezes; it's hard to see it against the early morning gloom and backdrop of eucalyptus trees. After a while I wonder whether I imagined it.

We drive to school via one of the stretches of Bells Beach, where they are setting up grandstands on the cliff-top for the world surfing championships. Down below, the sand is rich and golden, and quite dark, like burnt toffee. There are surfers already trying their luck on mountainous waves. Looking at this scene, I realise I still haven't metabolised the sense of travelling from one end of the world to the other, from cosy Ireland to a huge continent; but somehow now, gazing at the vast ocean, and the beach and the cliffs, I feel, not just think, I'm in Australia.

> A tick of a surfer—
> the mane of a wave
> shaking him off.

When we arrive at school I am whisked off to a 9.30 lesson of sixth formers. It feels far too early for cognitive functions, especially after a night of talking and wining. I don't know what to expect: will the kids be brash, bright, curious, cheeky? I assume they will have avoided poetry as much as possible. Poetry at my school was definitely considered off-limits and foppish by the pupils. And here in sunny, outdoor sporty Australia?

The classroom fills up. A mixture of girls and boys, the girls wearing pale summer dresses, the boys grey shorts and pale shirts, all clean-cut, wholesome. Claire is there to hold my hand and facilitate. I think of Yeats's: 'the children's eyes / In momentary wonder stare upon / A sixty-year-old smiling public man'. I can feel myself smiling involuntarily: I come from the Planet Poetry and I mean you no harm.

I say a few words about myself and hand out a selection of eight poems I've put together to show the variety of poetry. A haiku, an Anglo-Saxon riddle, William Blake, a concrete poem by Roger McGough, etc. They seem to be interested, or some do, and Claire jollies them along. The lesson is fifty minutes long and towards the end I am flagging. Wine and lingering jet lag have meshed together. The bell goes in the nick of time.

Claire takes me to the staffroom, where sixty euphoric teachers are milling around with cups of tea and crowding over a sumptuous food trolley with ham sandwiches and superior quiche.

> Brea-
> k
> time, a biscuit
> snapped!

Announcements are made and cheery Lloyd introduces me to the whole room—a school ritual for visitors. I'm willing him on to shout, 'Well, what have we here!', but no such luck and I am simply obliged to stand up and receive hearty applause. What a great reaction to just standing up. If only poetry readings could be like that.

Various teachers come up to say hello to me—all of them unstuffy and friendly. Australians, like the Irish, seem to remember they're human beings first, professionals second.

A bell goes, teachers drift away, and my collywobbles drift in. The second lesson is with the Lower Sixth, a larger and slightly younger group than the first. Claire is again full of verve and energy, inviting the pupils to split into twos to discuss the poems, inviting pairs of them to jot notes on the whiteboard. There's so much more physical movement and discussion than I recall from my schooldays, when we sat, heads down, not daring to move, speak, eyes pretending to stare at differential equations or the Aeneid, praying our names wouldn't be called out and that the clock would accelerate. They students warm to the Anglo-Saxon riddle in particular.

> I saw four creatures   —curious they were—
> moving as one,   making dark tracks,
> prints of pure black.   Its progress was swift,
> faster than birds   it flew through the air,
> dived under water.   The tenacious warrior,
> working unceasingly,   showed all four of them
> the way they must go   across gleaming gold.

We have fun trying to guess the answer. Eventually I give a visual clue, borrowing a pencil from one of the pupils and holding it up. Someone gets it: three fingers and a quill. Those are the 'four creatures', leaving dark tracks of ink, moving through air and diving into the inkhorn ('water'), guided by a tenacious arm to a manuscript with gold leaf.

The bell goes and we rise to our feet, float up and away, as if invisible weights have been untied from our feet.

> School bell once again:
> each reflex red alert—
> late, late, sorry sir I'm late.

Claire drives me off to the tiny station and I catch an afternoon train back to Melbourne, emerging at Southern Cross onto a street of office workers scuttling through the evening shadows of skyscrapers. The tram north to Fitzroy is almost second nature, the Myki card snug in my hand.

At home, Sappho is waiting for me with a litany of meows. I top up her bowl with her pellets and sling a nob of meat onto the backyard; she advances like a Coliseum lion, then sits on her haunches, a riddle wrapped up in a sphinx.

The house is shady and cool, the sofa soft, the room quiet. I'm off-duty. Silence. Heaven. Break-time.

The Southern Cross

The next morning, Wednesday, marks my being in Australia for almost a week, and I still haven't put pen to paper. It feels like a Rubicon moment, and I make the decision not to write at all but instead meet as many people as I can and do as much as possible. I can write anywhere, but I might never return to Australia, which is both a liberating and poignant thought.

Today I have been invited to have lunch at the university with Kevin, along with Amanda and Denise, who are associated with the Vincent Buckley Prize. Kevin has also promised to give me a guided tour of the campus. Then in the evening I am having supper locally in Fitzroy at the house of Martin, a friend of a Dublin poet friend back home.

I walk to the university along quiet back roads; a few deep-fried autumnal leaves are crinkling up on the tarmac, but the streets are flooded with light, and everyone's dressed in frocks, shorts and sandals. There are so many cafés spilling onto the pavements that you could breeze from one to another all day long, all year long, and never return to your starting point.

I wait at my rendezvous, one of the many campus gates, and watch crowds of students hurry past to lecture halls, faculty buildings, libraries. After a while my eye catches two women coming towards me, one with hair piled up, the other with straight blonde locks. They're both staring at me and laughing. Is it my super-cool hat? When in earshot, one calls out: 'We've just realised we know what you look like, but you haven't got the foggiest what we look like!' Amanda and Denise lead me off to the law building, a swish tower block with a restaurant on the tenth floor, soothingly carpeted, with sweeping views across the vast campus. Kevin soon joins us. I suspect he has just been to see his mother in hospital, and I wonder how she is, and how he is. He shows no signs of distress, but he seems the stoic type.

My three companions all order fish, which is 'snapper', and they all giggle after the young waiter unintentionally over-emphasises it—'We've got SNAPPER on the menu', as if it's a threat in case we walk off without paying. I have PASTA.

Conversation flows; one glass of white wine and I feel like the old Chinese poet Li Bai trying to reach the moon in lake water and tipsily falling in. Someone asks me what I think about the recent death of Martin McGuinness, the Irish IRA-man-turned-politician. I don't know what I think about it and withhold a platitudinous answer. The questioner mentions, smilingly, being brought up on tales of the 'British bayonetting babies' and being conditioned to hate Brits.

My inner Krishnamurti voice whispers that only by breaking cages of conditioning can we truly commune with one another. I remember a friend telling me how once, when visiting Auschwitz, he saw a busload of young German children arriving on a school trip. They were full of larky fun, boys and girls, whistling, giggling, some holding hands, glad to be out of school. My friend saw them an hour later, twelve-year-olds trailing along with sad bowed faces, the weight of German history suddenly on their backs—for the rest of their lives. Does history enlighten? Or condition or embitter?

I'm guessing that one of Australia's, or Melbourne's, strengths is, or should be, the erosion of ancestral national prejudices. There seem to be so many people of mixed heritage that it would surely make it harder to preserve bigotries inherited from the Old World. Which is not to say that nationalistic feelings won't transfer themselves to different types of chauvinism. How hard it is to give up the emotions that come with being raised a Catholic, Muslim, atheist,

Scot or Australian. Let alone a West Ham United supporter. As a Wolves-supporting friend told me, with great sadness: 'You can change your house, change your wife, even change your gender. But you can't change your football team.'

After lunch Kevin gives me a speedy tour of the campus. We wander along tree-lined paths, through grassy squares and past huge new buildings, stylish faculties of architecture, arts and law. I feel nostalgic for learning, research, and the endless possibilities of youth—all those things I ignored when I was at university, where instead of reading English literature I escaped into reading the bottle labels of cheap sherry.

Kevin finishes the tour with a visit to a famous Italian cake shop, Brunetti, in Lygon Street.

> Student faces rushing past
> future-rapt;
> my cone of ice cream melting.

I arrive back home in Fitzroy. I shower, change, stroke Sappho and give her some deep psychotherapeutic counselling along the lines of: 'Don't worry, I'll be back later,' then head out to visit the friend of a friend.

Martin lives up the road in a typical Victorian house, single-fronted, narrow, but stretching back to a walled garden. We talk above the hiss of a stir-fry which he prods and adjusts. He is curious to know what I think of Australia, while I am curious to know about relations between white Australians and the Indigenous peoples.

I am not sure what I think about Australia. I've only been here a few days. I tell him how we used to study the country in primary school and mention that my school was called Wallop. He thinks I'm joking, then role-plays being the Chair of the school-naming committee: 'Shall we choose Thwack-'em or Wallop? Okay, let's have Wallop—that will attract the parents!' I tell him that the headmaster was a big, kind man called Colonel Amyas Biss and that his sausage dog Cosy would join our lessons half way through them. We would hear a scratching at the door, and Biss would bellow, 'Someone let that wretched dog in!' Cosy, old and rotund, would click her way in and lie on top of Biss's shoes, or, more usually, his slippers. Martin hugs himself with delight at this Dickensian tale.

But what to make of Australia, apart from sunny first impressions in cosmopolitan Melbourne? In some ways it seems quite Asian—the climate, the number of Chinese, Vietnamese, Filipino and Thai faces on the street; and I remember Kevin saying that Australians don't give a thought about Britain and the country's British origins. But everywhere there are reminders of it. You pick up a dollar coin and it has a kangaroo on one side and Queen Elizabeth II on the other. The streets are called Gresham, Bond, Manchester, Royal, Union, William, and so on. The older houses could be from a seaside town in Lancashire or Kent. Multicultural loyalism?

And the white Australians I have met do seem to have a deep-seated unease about the Indigenous peoples. It strikes me that it must be surreal living in a country in which two different cultures live side by side, one still in touch with its prehistoric roots, the other advancing fair into a technological nirvana. It would be akin to, mutatis mutandis, the modern Scots living alongside the ancient Picts. In such a scenario, the Scots would surely profit from insights into an ancient culture. But I'm not sure how much the Picts would benefit. Better health care, certainly. But they would lament their children being drawn from millennia-old traditional songs, dances, and rituals into the world of social media and smartphones. They might well experience a 'loss of soul' and turn to cheap whisky.

Martin tells me that white Australia is predicated on water, which exists only along the rim of the country. No water, no white Australia. The Indigenous peoples want respect, he says, but it's hard for white people to know how to give or show it. Money and investment in facilities haven't worked. I mention that Kevin says literacy is the key. No one can effect change without a voice. Martin agrees.

After supper he takes me outside to see his backyard. It's dark but the stars are out. I tell him that the one constellation I'm dying to see is the Southern Cross, a name that has exerted its magic on me for as long as I can remember. He looks up, swivels, and there it is, at the end of an invisible extension of his finger. The sky has a film of mist but I can see the stars and match them with those on the Australian flag. They fit.

In 1891 Rudyard Kipling published a patriotic poem called 'The English Flag', which includes this verse:

'My basking sunfish know it, and wheeling albatross,
Where the lone wave fills with fire beneath the Southern Cross.
What is the Flag of England? Ye have but my reefs to dare,
Ye have but my seas to furrow. Go forth, for it is there!'

Two years later, Banjo Patterson wrote 'Our Own Flag', which includes this verse:

'The English flag may flutter and wave,
where the world wide oceans toss
but the flag the Australian dies to save
is the flag of the Southern Cross.'

Martin suddenly hears a noise and whispers: 'There's a possum on the wall!' I am thrilled. I still haven't seen a live adult possum in motion. It's difficult to see into the branches of the tree in front of us, but I do spot what looks like the outline of a creature. It doesn't move. We don't move. We linger for a while and go inside.

I don't stay much longer and when I leave there's a coolness in the air and a slight autumnal wind brushing the trees. The season is changing at last.

> Garden wall at night—possum!
> The eyes of the Southern Cross
> burning.

Footy for thought

Thursday. I'm woken rudely by a loud thump—not the possum this time, but the javelin of a rolled-up newspaper. This is the way the day begins, not with a whimper but a bang.

I know I have stuff on today, but I can't remember what it is. I look at my schedule. 'Seminar on "poetry and imagination" at university, 3 pm.' Hmm, that sounds really interesting; the sort of thing I'd love to go to.

Then I realise that it's me giving the seminar. Heart gives a thump like a rolled-up newspaper slapping a bedroom window. A morning to rehearse.

Next item on my scribbled list of notes is: 'Footy in the evening'. Kevin is taking me to an Australian Rules football match as part of my education. It's a local Melbourne derby between two teams who take their names from city districts: Carlton (Kevin's team) and Richmond. It's the opening match of the season. I imagine this will mean a bumper crowd of about 25,000 people, but Kevin says it's being held at the Melbourne Cricket Ground and more than 70,000 are expected. I find it hard to believe that a Carlton and Richmond derby will have the same amount of support as, say, matches between Real and Athletico Madrid, Inter and AC Milan, or Manchester City and Manchester United.

I'm not sure what to expect at my seminar. The organiser wasn't specific about subject matter and hazy about numbers of students, types of student, etc. I like to prepare things to death, cover all eventualities, so I whirl through my notes like a dervish.

After lunch I set off to the university and arrive in good time. The seminar is being held in a small upstairs faculty room with a table and a few chairs. Five people turn up: two students, Kevin, his poet friend and colleague Grant, and the organiser. The two students are doing PhDs in creative writing. One of them is a big, burly, friendly man with a ponytail, in his fifties; the other is American, late twenties, suave and confident. I'm not sure whether the small turn-out makes me feel more, or less, relaxed.

More relaxed it turns out—I feel able to talk, almost without notes. I touch on 'imagination', Charles Harpur, William Blake's 'Double Vision', and other matters. After I have finished, the ponytailed man says he is struck by my mentioning that Michael Foot, an old British Labour MP, said that Margaret Thatcher had no imagination, 'and therefore no compassion'. It's certainly a damning judgement. I'm not sure it's true—that people who are apparently 'low in imagination' can't be compassionate. There are probably different types of imagination. The sort that allows you to come up with new ideas and words, and the sort that allows you to empathise with people and therefore want to help them. People talk about 'emotional intelligence'; but perhaps there's also an 'emotional imagination'. Nurses may not be artistically imaginative, but they often exude extraordinary empathy in my experience.

After the session we disband. Kevin goes off to a memorial service reception and I, basking in post-seminar euphoria, go to a small sandwich bar on the fringes of the campus, where I will wait for Kevin to pick me up. I have a recuperative cup of tea then decamp to a small nearby patch of grass, where there is an inviting bench. I lie on it like a dosser; the air is warm and the sky is clear of thoughts.

> Smoke-map of clouds:
> New Zealand vaporises
> into the land of the long blue ocean.

Kevin arrives and we take a tram to Federation Square—Melbourne's unofficial city centre, a buzzy concrete space with strollers, sightseers, outdoor music, etc. We walk to the MCG and Kevin is preoccupied by his mum, who faces an operation on the morrow.

The stadium is huge and its forecourt displays bronze statues of cricketing greats in action poses. We wade through long queues of fans—the Richmond ones ('the Tigers') are dressed in yellow and black, the Carlton ones in dark blue—and find our seats. We sit adjacent to a group of hard-core Richmond supporters, some with painted stripy faces or wearing tiger costumes, waving a variety of banners, yellow 'car-wash' dusters and yellow bowler hats. Kevin bemoans that Carlton are going through a 'period of rebuilding'. I say: 'Which is another way of saying they're useless?' 'Yeh.'

I had forgotten what it was like to be in a huge arena. The empty spaces dotted around the stadium miraculously fill up; phone-cameras flicker and glitter from the ranks of more than 70,000 folk. The pre-match rituals are an anthropologist's dream: official supporters of each team take to the pitch and unveil a huge rice-paper banner bearing a cheeky slogan to taunt the rival supporters, such as 'Tigers are toothless. Go, Carlton!' The teams then come out and have to run through their respective banners, smashing them to pieces. Fireworks cascade and huge TV screens pan in on the faces of the players. Each team has its own special anthem, which is blasted out of loudspeakers with a benign jauntiness. The blend of brassy melody and cheesy unison singing resembles theme tunes from 1960s American TV comedies such as 'I Love Lucy' or 'The Flintstones'.

The match itself is Wagnerian in length—four quarters of roughly thirty minutes, i.e. about two hours—but not in drama: Richmond are far too powerful and send our neighbouring fans into yellow ecstasies, like lemon trees in Seville during a storm. By contrast, venting their frustration, the two middle-aged Carlton-supporting women next to me shriek like crows dowsed with boiling water, to the extent that I have to stick a finger in my left ear.

The match itself has a terrific pulsing rhythm that's more like that of Gaelic football or basketball—end to end, fast paced—than that of soccer or rugby.

After the match we leave with the hordes and join the Melbourne dusk; hundreds are still milling around Federation Square, chatting, drinking, lighting up cigarettes. I feel I've had an authentic glimpse of Australia—the hybrid marsupial-like game, the totemic symbols (teams are called Tigers, Cats, Swans, etc.), the innocent pre-match rituals, the good cheer of the supporters. I can't imagine footy ever being like soccer in 1970s Britain, my peak period of interest, when gangs of skinheads wearing braces and Doc Martens—'bovver boots'—made you fear for your life. I remember when as a young lad my dad took me to West Ham v Spurs for my birthday in December. After the match we had to travel back by tube train in a carriage packed tight with skinheads, all chewing gum and snarling. My dad and I got separated in the heaving squash of braced bodies. And I'll never forget the moment when our tube stop arrived and my dad turned round, flustered, and shouted across to me, 'Come along Beezlebugs, we've got to get off here!' Why he had to use a variation on my family nickname ('Boo') still remains a mystery, but I still shudder at the sudden collective twitch among the skinheads as they looked around to see who 'Beezlebugs' was. I slipped through the testosteronic phalanx like a spider down a plughole and made it to safety.

We take a tram to Brunswick and go our separate ways, Kevin cycling, me walking twenty minutes through dark leafy backstreets to Fitzroy. Tomorrow Kevin is going off to a folk festival with his two kids, but under the cloud of his mum. I shall be Kevin-less for the weekend, which will seem strange.

I enter my house. Sappho asks me who won. She's glad, for some strange reason, that it was the Tigers.

Match post mortem—
stadium filling with ghosts
of those who cannot leave.

Fine dining

Friday morning. I've been in Australia for just over a week and I haven't gone back on my decision not to write. Things must be going well! Today I have another lunch at the university and, in the evening, I shall be wined and dined in downtown Melbourne by Claire and Strazz—two of the teachers from the school I visited.

By now I know the backstreets to the university and I arrive there in perfect time to meet a high-powered scientist, a contact given to me from someone back home. She is in her sixties, short, grey-haired, formally dressed in a grey skirt and jacket, perhaps a bit geed up at meeting a stranger from a faraway country, a stranger who is also geed up to meet a high-powered scientist. When she asks me why I'm here in Melbourne, I venture a feeble joke: 'Oh. I went to Singapore and got the wrong plane and stayed.' Instead of emitting a short humouring laugh, she looks concerned, as if I'm going to be hard on myself. She touches me lightly on the arm and with big sympathetic eyes says: 'Oh, no, no, that's a very easy thing to do …' I then have to explain I was being droll, and feel foolish. A bad start.

But after more gentle mutual probings, the formality begins to loosen. She tells me that she was raised in the country and her primary school consisted of being taught how to catch eels in streams, as well as how to snare and skin snakes and hang them up on washing lines.

'You actually did that?'

'Oh, yeah. Hundreds of times. But when I got to secondary school that's all I could do. I had no grammar or spelling.'

I think of my primary school and the life skills we learned: playing conkers and learning smutty jokes.

She is interested in my perspective on Australia and my poetry gigs; for some reason we get onto religion. I find myself explaining Zen Buddhism to her and what a Zen 'riddle', or koan, is. She likes the sound of 'one hand clapping', or the lack of it. This leads me on to Anglo-Saxon riddles and medieval history, and then I tell her about learning history at school and my headmaster called Amyas Biss. His unusual name touches her funny bone and she gets unexpectedly giggly, her academic persona cracking round the edges. It's downhill from there. We share other people's unusual names and descend into wine-aided, barely controlled hysteria; she can hardly get the words out to tell me of a surgeon she knows called Mr Butcher. I mention a Chinese dentist called Mr Phang. I then say it's like the book, Cliff Tragedy by Eileen Dover, a joke, amazingly, she hasn't heard before. She rocks in her chair, tears in her eyes, and I decide it best to hold back on Jungle Tragedy by Claude Balls.

We have become new best friends in the space of an hour or so.

Eventually, with a warm giggly handshake I head back to Fitzroy, which increasingly feels like an ancestral home.

> Backyard sunshine;
> Sappho licking
> the furry drumstick of herself.

I shower, rest, then 'tram it down'—a phrase that is now part of my vocabulary—to the bright lights of the city centre with that old Friday evening, freedom-from-the-office scent in my nostrils. Friday evening / night has always been, will always be, the best few hours of the week. I meet Claire and Strazz in one of the swishest Italian restaurants in town, or indeed anywhere.

Strazz, it turns out, is of Italian stock, and his folk had helped to establish the restaurant back in the day, so he's treated like royalty, with lots of hugs with the cook and staff. We are chaperoned into the magnificent dining room on the first floor; chandeliers and Giotto-style murals give it the air of a Doge's residence. The waiters glide across the carpet on invisible skates and have the arm movements of tai chi teachers, responding to your every twitch: I happen to sneeze and the movement of my head is enough to bring a waiter hurrying over.

We have a series of small but exquisite dishes—a something stuffed with a something else and garnished with herbs I've never tasted before. I have risotto for one course, small, perfectly seasoned, and accompanied by a Mount Etna wine, recommended by the young wine waiter who, it turns out, was once taught by Claire at school. I wonder whether it might be a bit of a comedown for a well-educated lad in his late twenties to be waiting at table—until he lets slip that he is also running his own wine-importing business.

Strazz is in his element; he has a comfortable waistline and silvery curly hair, and is liveried in a pale jacket complemented by a bright tie. His fingers are fluttery and expressive, as he lets loose his eloquence on anecdotes, such as: finding himself in a backstreet Italian restaurant in New York, which turns out to be a mafia dive; guns are raised at him, then lowered when he offers his credentials by declaring that he's heard the chef makes the best tomato passata in the world. The aggression comes to a halt; someone shouts a name; a tense wait, and then the chef emerges and inaugurates Strazz into the family.

Then there's his story about almost being run over by Stephen Hawking in Cambridge. Emerging from a pub at night, Strazz saw headlights coming towards him on the pavement—he quickly realised it was a power-chair that wasn't going to stop. Jumping out of the way in the nick of time he saw, as the vehicle sped past, Stephen Hawking behind the controls: 'I was furious. I shouted at him, "You effing bastard, watch where you're effing going!" I was going to run after him but he was too quick. Gone in a flash.'

After Strazz's brief history of (almost) crime, the pudding arrives: a light, intense chocolate soufflé with a tiny scoop of ice cream and small jug of melted chocolate sauce; with coffee comes a blood-orange segment dipped in chocolate and topped with herbs. No porridge with frogs' legs here.

We say goodbye outside in the warm autumn air—all merry and huggy among the city lights, the milling night-goers and passing trams, and go our separate ways. As Yeats said: 'Our souls are love and a continual farewell.'

Bombed out

My second Saturday morning in Australia. I have overslept and stumble out at 10.30 am, greeted by sulky Sappho, understandably wanting her food. I go to the fridge, choose a ration of meat and toss it onto the sunlit backyard brickwork, make tea and toast for myself, then we both tuck into our brunches harmoniously.

I realise I have no appointments, no meetings, no gigs, for the first time since arriving. As soon as the brain has confirmed this, the body sags. I feel as if I could sit on the sofa all day.

Which is exactly what I do, revelling in stasis, becoming the navel I am gazing at, or reading my book on Charles Harpur, settling into his life and poems. Sappho creaks in and out of the room, sometimes settling down to snooze, sometimes pottering. We look at each other from time to time and I am suddenly reminded of a ninth-century Irish poem called 'Pangur Bán' ('Pangur the white cat'), about a monk and his cat going about their separate lives but being companionable. It's well known in Ireland and poets often try their hands at writing versions of it. This is mine:

Pangur Bán

My white cat Pangur and myself
Have each our specialist skill—
I catch thoughts, ideas and words
He tracks rodents for the kill.

The world of vellum, ink and pen
Brings me joy much more than fame;

And Pangur doesn't envy me,
Enraptured by his jolly game.

At home we're like two kindred souls
Never bored and having fun,
Immersed in our respective callings
Joined together but … alone.

Sometimes a mouse will creep along
And he'll snatch it from behind;
Sometimes a thought will just dart up
And I will seize it in my mind.

He sets his steady brilliant eye
To scan a wall or other surface;
While I stare feebly at a page
To make myself more wise and learned.

Whenever he ensnares a mouse
He cries triumphantly *miaow*!
When I unpick a mental knot
I silently exclaim *hurray*!

Although we are companions
We let each other work in peace
And focus on our different arts—
Me on words, and him on mice.

Pangur … is Master of the Rodent,
Has honed his craft for years untold;
And I, too, labour at my trade
To turn base metal into gold.

When I check my mails there's one from Kevin saying that his folk festival is going well and that while driving there, a huge kangaroo had sprung out and crossed the road just in front of him; if he'd been driving any faster … He also says he is giving a lecture on haiku on

Monday and I can come to it if I want. I do so want.

Kangaroo haiku:
the syllables hop, hop, hop—
jump.

The evening seeps in and I've barely stirred from the sofa. I turn on the telly and there's an Aussie Rules match on. A week ago I would have switched channels automatically, but now that I see the green turf of the MCG and feel the adrenaline coursing through the packed stadium, I dream myself back to my own evening there, and I'm riveted.

The Essendon Bombers are playing the Hawthorn Hawks, both Melbourne teams. The Bombers were apparently found guilty of using illegal supplements a few years back and excluded from the 2013 finals; the club was fined $2 million and players were suspended. This match sees the return of six of their suspended players, and their supporters are delirious with potential redemption against the mighty Hawks. As the Bombers race onto the pitch, one of their directors begins cranking up a hand-operated siren, like an old-fashioned air-raid warning, and it howls through the stadium.

The Bombers have the usual Aussie Rules giant orcs, but also a terrific dread-locked Indigenous player, who seems lilliputian compared with the colossi charging up and down the field, but who, to quote a newspaper about another Indigenous player, 'moves like liquid'. The Bombers are too charged with a natural supplement—testosterone—to be resisted, and eventually the Hawks are grounded by twenty-five points.

Day of rest:
nothing doing,
doing nothing.

The State of Origen

Sunday is a return to activity. This time it's a rendezvous with a stranger, another friend of a friend, a medievalist named Constant, whom I'm to meet at the Thresherman's Bakehouse, near the Italian quarter in Carlton, a place he frequents with friends after Sunday mass. Our mutual poet friend, Hilary, has briefed me about him, and everything sounds good: a multilingual, multidisciplinary medieval historian and a world expert on Abelard and Héloïse, but interested in almost everything, including Irish saints, a passion of mine.

I arrive in good time. The Bakehouse has tables outside on the pavement; the interior, with its high ceiling and wood surrounds, has the feel of a cricket pavilion.

I suspect that the senior gents and ladies sitting at a long table might be part of Constant's group, but there's no sign of him. I could of course go up to one of them and ask the obvious question, but I'm too shy. Instead I sit outside and eke out a coffee. Finally, I spot him, with his wife, hurrying along. About my age, shortish, slightly cherubic face, ambling gait. I spring up like Stanley: 'Constant, I presume?' He is amazed I know what he looks like and is delighted to meet me, as is his wife Maryna, a softly-spoken New Zealander. Constant takes me in and introduces me to his companions at the table. I'm greeted like an old friend, and everyone wants to know how I'm finding Australia and Melbourne. They all talk at once and I field questions like slip catches, dropping some and bagging others.

Constant and I then get down to business, establishing basics. He speaks quickly, jumping from subject to subject, as I imagine

Abelard used to. He asks me what sort of poetry I write and, on cue, I pull out two of my books. One features a series on Irish saints and he is delighted to see a poem on St Carthage, a little-known figure who happens to be the patron saint of his local church. The other book is passed round and one woman excitedly pushes it towards me, prodding at an open page: 'Can you read this please?' I don't really fancy reading anything aloud in a café, but I look at the poem and it's one entitled 'Origen'—about the not-very-well-known early theologian who is said to have castrated himself—the very subject, in fact, of the poem. It doesn't seem seemly to read the poem while others around us are eating their … boiled eggs and avocado salads. I play for time: 'Not sure I'm up to reading this—haven't read it since I wrote it years ago.'

I then ask, in a doubtful tone, if anyone happens to know about Origen. I have fallen into the trap. Ten heads nod in unison as ten hands go up. They all studied him the previous week, stupid! I have no choice. I launch myself into the poem and get a round of applause for my troubles. They are the most informed audience I have ever had, or will ever have. It's strange to think that nearly two thousand years after Origen performed his act of self-mutilation, a poem about it would be read aloud in a café in a continent he would have been astounded to know existed at the other side of the world.

Origen

The slow awakening of summer
Courtyards of Alexandria again
Adrip with bundled honeysuckle
A wine cup warming in the sun
Such sweetness from the Song of Songs!
Let him kiss me with the kisses
Of his mouth.
                    Unbearable
The season and the rising flood
Of love, unbearable the stench

Of ripeness in the groins, a ripeness
That pushes him, a harvesting—
And relief, one sickle-moon slash
Two tiny worlds cupped in his hand.

As we get up to disperse, Maryna invites me to come back next week and suggests a jaunt to an out-of-town art gallery called Heide, a place I've been meaning to go to. We part with good cheer and I head off to the university library.

Origen,
Abelard—
ballsy thinkers.

En route to the library I happen to meet one of the two students who came to my seminar, David, the friendly ponytailed one; we have a brief chat and afterwards I feel unnaturally elated—from the illusory sense that I can walk the streets of Melbourne and bump into people I know.

I proceed to the university's Baillieu Library and try to figure out the book loan system; a librarian talks me through it, managing to be instructive, non-patronising and humorous; that's been one of the striking things about Australia—the unforced charm and helpfulness of shop and other assistants. They seem to be universally cheerful, but not in a conditioned customer-service way.

I get a book out on Charles Harpur then thread my way through the paths of the campus, which has a Sunday calm before the Monday.

I head east towards Fitzroy, stopping en route at the Potter Museum, a boutique gallery space. The current exhibition has nineteenth-century landscape paintings—romanticised mountain, forest or panoramic harbour scenes, sometimes with Indigenous peoples sliding into the foreground, or dancing around in the background, to give a dash of 'local colour'. I'm struck by the paintings of John Glover, who instinctively pits the grandeur of Australian topography—towering tree-covered hills and broad plains—against little human beings and their puny dwellings. I can feel the vast continental space through Glover's work, which, even at one remove, tests my tolerance for boundlessness.

Back inside my cosy enclosed home, Sappho is lying in the shade of the courtyard. It is twenty-eight degrees and we're both fit for nothing but flopping. I make a cup of tea and turn on the TV to see what's happening in the world. Shaun the Sheep, one of our family favourites, is on. The farmer is picking juicy apples from a tree and chucking them down to his dog, Bitzer, with Shaun trying to steal them from under his nose. Shirley, the huge sheep, keeps sneezing and the force of the wind scatters the apples everywhere. I flick to ABC News 24, where the weather woman is announcing in grave tones that Queensland is braced for a cyclone that's been named Debbie. I remember that Queensland is where my cousin Louise, from Kildare, is living and I email her with concern. She soon replies cheerfully: she's not that anxious about Debbie and is about to go swimming with her two young children in the local lagoon. Where else?

> Cyclone
> approaching.
> Deep, deep
> breath …

Haiku

Monday morning. Kevin is back in town! I set off to the university to attend his lecture on haiku and meet him beforehand in his office. We walk down to a theatre in what's called the Old Electrical Engineering Building, in which I expect to see Dr Frankenstein cackling over a corpse-like creature wired up to a Van Der Graaf generator.

The lecture hall is packed; about sixty young undergrads, notepads open, pens twitching. It's novel to see Kevin in full professorial mode, relaxed, low key but authoritative. He has slides on a PowerPoint display and flashes up key concepts and examples of haiku. Bashō features, of course, and also Issa, who wrote one of my favourite poems:

> O Snail,
> climb Mt Fuji,
> but slowly, slowly.

The students scribble away, and I'm amazed at how much ground Kevin covers in fifty minutes. I wish I had a notebook too, but it's probably more Zen to let it wash over me. I mentally give him the sound of two hands clapping.

Afterwards we have lunch in a campus café and swap weekend news. While we do so it begins to bucket with rain; the Indian summer is breaking. Kevin hurries off to take a supervision and I head to the library, trying to shrink myself inside the radius of my brolly. I return the book on Charles Harpur and take out one by

John Bradley called *Singing Saltwater Country*, about the Indigenous 'songline' tradition, recommended to me by Constant.

I've always been interested in the roots of poetry. When did it all begin? Historians of language say that poetry preceded prose, because it's the language of memory. With its rhythms, repetitions, and images, poetry or poetic utterance was suited to memorise rituals and other traditional lore. But it's hard to know how extensive and universal poetry or verse was in prehistoric oral cultures. As George Steiner remarked, there must have been a moment in ancient Greece when someone stood on a cliff-top surveying the Aegean and said for the first time, 'that sea looks wine-dark'.

Perhaps the Indigenous communities, whose traditions go back tens of thousands of years, might shed some light on poetry, hence my resort to Bradley's book. The so-called 'songlines' are a sort of rhythmic, chanted 'poetry' or cousin of poetry: rapidly delivered, concentrated speech imbued, as it were, with sonic vibrations. The actual lines of the word 'songlines' refer to tracks across a landscape, said to be created by totemic ancestors such as Emu, or Dingo.

The journeys these ancestors took and what they did on them, whether making a camp fire or fighting a battle, explain the creation of topographical features, such as a waterhole, mountain, anthill, or rock. And the lines have a practical purpose too: marking boundaries of different tribal areas and providing signposts for crossing the desert.

Those are the 'lines' of the songlines. The 'songs' of the songlines celebrate and act out these ancestral journeys. What's interesting from the point of view of a modern poet is that the chanted songlines do not recall past events so much as make listeners feel as if they're actually participating in the narrative. It's the difference between being in a school history class about the battle of Gettysburg, and actually playing the part of a soldier in a historical re-enactment. To enchant members of an audience so that they feel part of the story must be the aim of all poets and artists.

In a songline of the Yanyuwa people of northern Australia, for example, as Bradley records, the words tell of the journey of the ancestor spirit Dingo. Part of it goes like this: 'Footprints of the Dingo / in the sand as he crosses / the sand-ridge country // Gravel lines the bed / of the Fletcher Creek // Dingo walks over the gravel / in the dry Fletcher Creek, / he climbs the bank // Dingo smells the wind / of the plains country as he travels …' Even in translation you can sense poetry—in the rhythm, and the repetition of images, both crucial to the act of memorisation, and also, incidentally, reminding us that for the Greeks, the Muses were the daughters of Mnemosyne, 'Memory'. And it's the singing or chanting that activates the words into their fullness of being; the subtle risings and fallings of the melody mimic the progress of Dingo in a way that the speaking voice cannot match. This might give modern poets food for thought: that the element of sonic resonance, with its vitalising vibrations, gives words a musicality that transforms them.

I'm ready to leave the library, but it's raining so hard that I'm reduced to making short dashes to various overhanging buildings, as if I'm dodging sniper fire. I finally get back to the house and it's like walking into the dryness and stillness behind the curtain of a giant waterfall.

> Scurrying in from rain:
> a sofa, thick dry carpet,
> soft footfall of a paw.

Later on, with the wind and rain still lathering the windows, I turn on the telly and see that Cyclone Debbie is now careering into the edge of Queensland. Trees are bent double in seaside resorts. Waves the size of houses rear up from the sea. In various danger spots, local politicians and police chiefs, hunched outside in ferocious winds, urge people to leave their homes because of the threat of roof-wrenching gales and brimming rivers. I've never lived anywhere vulnerable to extreme weather conditions and say a prayer for Louise and her family.

In bed, impatient for sleep;
rain
drumming its fingers.

Gig

Tuesday is bright and warm again, as if the rain never happened.

I go shopping in the morning, bossing the Coles supermarket with growing confidence. I am feeding Kevin and myself before our big gig at the local Irish bar in the evening; we're both reading our poems in between two music acts.

I've been hesitant about this gig ever since Kevin first suggested it. I've done readings in bars before, and it's hard to feel tranquil in the face of tables of drinkers, people coming in and out, going to the toilets, ordering drinks, dodgy acoustics, and so on. But he was reassuring: not so much a bar, he said, as a café; lovely people running it; the clientele will be mostly his university students and a few friends; nice music acts to perform with.

And yet … the scars of bar-gigs run deep. As I told Kevin, the Blue Parrot Cocktail Bar in Brighton, England, in the mid-1990s was the nadir. Almost every poet I know has performed to an audience of only a couple of people, and sometimes nobody. But at this gig I performed in front of a negative audience.

I was due to read with an Irish poet friend called Martina Evans as part of the Brighton fringe festival. When we arrived at the bar, there were a few drinkers but nobody there for the poetry; the young organiser was mortified, blaming a breakdown in communication, lack of publicity, etc. Quick-witted but ill-advised, she approached a group of sloshed cocktail drinkers at the back of the room, about six of them, and bribed them with cocktails to be the audience. I can recall reading a rather emotional sonnet sequence about the death of my father, and seeing out of the corner of my eye, pie-eyed faces smirking, grinning, or staring into lurid-coloured drinks adorned with mini umbrellas.

'Won't be like that,' Kevin said.

He arrives in Fitzroy at about 5 pm on his trusty bike. I've put a quiche in the oven and made a Greek salad. He is quite weary, having just been to see his poorly mum, who is stable but feeling the effects of the anaesthetic from her operation.

After supper, we set off to the bar and there is no one there, apart from members of the four-piece band, Black Forest Smoke, and the barman, an engaging fella from County Cavan.

We wait half an hour and a few people drift in. By the time the band starts up there are about twenty-five people, mostly friends of Kevin. The band is excellent, fronted by Myron, an Aussie Ukrainian in his mid-sixties, tall, lots of dark hair, and with a similar singing style to Ian Dury of Blockheads fame. He half-growls his songs like a rottweiler with a sore throat. One of them goes: 'I knew I'd lost my temper when I set fire to the cushions.' Another one incorporates famous death-bed lines from history. His band includes a blonde, smiley, pig-tailed flautist, who balances Myron's gravitas with her light, enchanting trills. The only bad thing about the band, who reap rapturous applause after each song, is that I have to follow them.

And so it comes to pass … Kevin stands up and introduces me; my butterflies redouble. I've agonised for weeks over what to read. Definitely not my long poem about St Symeon Stylites sitting on top of a column for thirty years in the middle of the Syrian desert. Probably not the death of my father. If only I had lighter, chuckle-worthy poems for an occasion like this. I decide to read just four poems, all with an Irish theme, and to give them long intros—audiences always prefer intros to poems, and epigraphs to poems. Anything but poems. The microphone isn't the best and the full-frontal lighting doesn't help my straining eyes. The room has gone horribly silent. Jeez, they're waiting for me to open my mouth …

… Suddenly there's another burst of clapping: it's done. I have read the poems and already the healing alchemy of oblivion is working.

There is an interval. Kevin introduces me to a woman—I don't catch her name and ask her this and that, and how long her family has been in Australia, etc. I can't believe that her replies match the circumstances of Kevin's own family so precisely, and I'm about to report this amazing coincidence to him, when I suddenly realise she is his sister. She has just come from hospital, having seen their mum.

Kevin is next up on stage. He does a fine set, poems that have depth and humour, and his intros are well judged. By this time the second musical act has literally sneaked in—a certain Pete R, guitarist and songwriter. Pete follows Kevin straightaway and reveals that he is of Sicilian extraction and a solicitor. He apologises for being late—the reason being that he has only just got rid of his last client. Not really a Mick Jagger sort of excuse? He is in his sixties, big black-framed glasses, and seemingly as intense as his songs, which are in the tradition of Bob Dylan and Leonard Cohen. I enjoy the dexterity of his finger-picking and soulful voice, which has the right amount of lugubriousness.

Afterwards we linger for a short while, drink triple shots of vodka, fight off the groupies, smash up the bar, abuse passers-by, and get arrested for cocaine. Yeah, dream on. Me and Kevin stroll off to my place like two old birdwatchers after a day of medium success.

Back home, Kevin doesn't linger and sails off into the night.

I slump in front of the telly. More scary shots of Cyclone Debbie: palm trees with hair like giant Maenads, and a huddle of news reporters, coddling microphones as rain crashes down around their ears.

> Poetry reading;
> may you be here, this time,
> whoever you are.

Communicating

Wednesday. Kevin has invited me to go to a university seminar about modern literature given by two academics. Having not been in an academic seminar for a long time, if ever, I am curious to know what happens. I feel like an undercover agent.

We join a room of about thirty people sitting round a circle of arranged tables. The main speaker starts off, giving an introduction, and after fifteen minutes I realise I've barely grasped a word of what he is saying. It's most disconcerting, like walking into the future and hearing an evolved, scientific hybrid of the English language. I used to teach English to adults with learning difficulties, including dyslexia, and now I know how it feels to hear words and keep thinking I've misheard them. It must be some sort of karma, revenge for taking the English language for granted for too long.

I sense myself drifting.

Through the window, past the speaker's right ear, I can see students wandering past. Three girls of Indian extraction, late teens I guess, are holding hands and revolving slowly on the grass, beside an old tree; it's hard to know whether it's a dance, a ritual or a bit of fun. I drift back and hear words such as 'narratavising'—as if the words I've known since I was knee-high to a grasshopper have suddenly embraced an extra syllababble. Other words are familiar, but they appear in phrases that make me lose confidence: 'socialising the hegemony'; 'the hegemony of the oikos'; 'embedded sociability'. It's like being back in Mr Dunnett's maths class at school, praying not to be asked what dy over dx is. I leave the room feeling that my eyes have expanded, and my heart retracted.

> Through the seminar window,
> three girls dancing on grass—
> words have two left feet.

While Kevin goes off to a supervision, I take refuge in a nearby café, sitting outside at a small pavement table beside a busy main road. I luxuriate in open air, watching the multi-coloured trams and not having to concentrate. My euphoria manifests itself as a general smile to the world, like a jam jar designed to trap wasps: sure enough, a passing man, grey-haired and unshaven, catches my eye and straightway comes to sit at my tiny table, shaking my hand. I can tell from the start that he's disturbed; partly his slightly trampish appearance, but also the way he starts telling me his life story without preamble.

He says that he is British, living in Australia since the 1970s. He rambles on and I deduce that he is a manual labourer but used to be a boxer. More disconcerting is the way he suddenly gets weepy and says, 'I didn't mean to kill her'. This is followed by a mood swing and a sense of anger coursing through his body. I hold eye contact and feel myself becoming as tense as a banjo string, ready to go into fight or flight mode; well, flight mode. He is well built, muscular, and does indeed look like an ex-boxer.

The tension eases slightly when he rambles off onto another subject, about life on building sites. But then he keeps returning to the phrase, 'I didn't mean to kill her' and starts clutching his forehead. It feels like he needs a priest or therapist to confess to, not some random smiley poet sitting at a café table. I suggest, feebly, that perhaps he should talk to someone, preferably not me. He carries on with his leap-frogging tale. I don't feel able to get up and march away—more through cowardice, as if a sudden movement would stir up an ant's nest of aggression in him.

I hatch a plan while he continues to bare his soul. I listen until there is a slight pause in his story, then I tell him as authoritatively as I can: 'Dr Johnson said, "It matters not how a man dies, but how he lives". It doesn't really relate to his outpourings, but it's just enough to stop him in his tracks. I spring to my feet, shake his hand, wish him luck and speed away. I immediately feel shabby, without really knowing why; perhaps just guilty that my life is so much better than his?

I return home and resume the hegemony of my oikos; Sappho is like a furry icon of normality and sanity. I shall miss her terribly when I leave Melbourne, which is now only a week away.

> O Sappho of relentless needs—
> each one's worth meowing for,
> piteously.

Out to launch

Thursday. I'm due to have lunch in Fitzroy with a Melbourne poet called Earl with whom I've communicated, infrequently, over a number of years. From his poems and messages I've imagined someone in their late sixties, jacket and grey trousers, spectacles. An academic sort, or librarian, quiet and safe. We've arranged to meet at a tram stop near my house at lunchtime, and I realise I should have asked him what he looks like—to stop me from over-staring at passers-by.

I keep thinking he will descend from a tram, but finally a man walks up to me from a different direction and sure enough, it's Earl. He turns out to be about my age, steely hair scraped back into a knotted pony tail, smiley face, glasses, quite stocky but fit-looking. We adjourn to a vegetarian café, a big noisy establishment with trestle tables, full of lunch-break workers. We sit at a small table and it's not long before my preconceived image of him, already shaken by his appearance, disappears altogether with his talk of having a black belt in jujitsu and being a guitarist.

He tells me about his Welsh ancestry and fascination with all things Arthurian, and I wonder whether the mythic imagination of European-descended Australians necessarily gravitates towards the old Western tales. Will there ever come a time when the stories of the Indigenous peoples become those of white Australians too? Otherwise there will always perhaps be a psychic split between the two communities, and a loss of soul for both sides. Mythic stories are rooted in the places of their genesis. It feels poignant to think of Earl driving through the blazing Australian outback, seeing in his mind's eye the misty mountains of Snowdonia.

We chat for a solid three hours. As I walk home, I marvel at the disparity between my preconceived image of him and the reality. I remember Krishnamurti saying that we should not only encounter strangers with an open frame of mind, but also our loved ones, because every time we meet them we are different from the last time we saw them, and they are different too. We all walk around with frozen images that we brand on the familiar.

Back home, Sappho doesn't seem at all different from this morning. She hasn't moved from where I left her. The glorious life of the cat! As for me, I have to leave again straightaway for the university, this time for an evening book launch. The poet with a new book is a woman called Jordie Albiston, a poem of whose Kevin had read to me some days before, and which I liked a lot.

I meet Kevin in his professorial office and we make our way through corridors and up stairs to a mezzanine area with large sheets of window glass dominating the walls. There's a familiar book launch buzz, with statutory glasses of white wine and peanuts, people talking at each other in twos and threes. It's like a cultural maternity ward, with everyone knowing what gender the baby is.

I'm feeling a bit lost, but Kevin introduces me to a swathe of cheery people, including Jordie herself, who looks the part of a radiant mother, and Christopher Wallace-Crabbe, the doyen of Australian poetry, who is going to launch the book with a speech.

The occasion takes me back to the launch of my first poetry book, at the Tower Bookshop in central London. My family were coming to it, some from far-off places, as well as friends and colleagues. I turned up at the shop half an hour early, all a-flutter, dying to see my debut book gleaming on the counter—it would be my first glimpse of it. I was met by my publisher's assistant, a young slip of a girl, who said: 'Slight problem, James. The books aren't quite here yet. Peter is picking them up from the printers now.' I couldn't believe it. The book had been in the pipeline for years. The launch date set for months. Complex travel arrangements had been made. I went off to the pub and drank a whisky.

On returning, I was amazed to see the shop jammed-pack with people—all reading the same book: mine. Among the guests was the uninvited Eddie Linden, a notorious Scottish literary figure who haunted the book launches of London. He was pale-complexioned, red-faced, wearing a navy beret, and very drunk. He was swaying into the guests, with one loud refrain on his lips: 'Are yooo a fockin' Tory?' His recipients either smiled, frowned, or backed away.

To my horror I could see him sway towards my dear little mum, a sheltered conservative with a capital and lower-case c. Sure enough, Eddie breathed his frumious refrain over her: 'Are yooo a fockin' Tory?' Mum didn't blink: 'Well, as a matter of fact I am.' Eddie was so shocked by the speed and honesty of her reply that he reeled back, as if hit by an electrical force.

With the clinking of a glass and contagious 'hushes' around the room, conversations splutter, stall and cut out. Christopher Wallace-Crabbe stands up and says a few well-chosen words. Jordie then takes centre stage, dispenses thanks to those who made the book possible and reads a few poems. The wine has sunk to the part of my brain that makes me feel united to everyone in the room and sentimentally conscious of the poet's life, the incessant struggle to get the words right, the meaning matching the music, to say something worthwhile, and to do it 'slantwise'; then the almighty struggle to get work published, sold, reviewed. T.S. Eliot never uttered a truer word when he said poetry was 'a mug's game'.

Eventually we disperse, clutching our books. Kevin rides off into the night on his two-wheeled steed, and I walk back home on my two-legged one.

As I enter the house there's meowing from the dark, and Sappho is waiting for me with a rolling pin.

Manners

Friday. Today I have a visitor coming for lunch, an old Irish friend of my cousin, Louise, who still seems to be surviving Cyclone Debbie up in Queensland. I tidy up and go out to Coles to buy lunch. I feel like an old customer there, with an honorary loyalty card.

Catherine arrives at 12.30, on her way to work, teaching English as a foreign language, mostly to Columbian women, she says, who need to improve their English to improve their chances of being allowed to stay permanently in the country. She's in her early thirties, at a guess, neat features, high forehead, long sheeny brown hair, quietly spoken, bright and witty. It's lovely to hear an Irish accent and to reminisce about Athy, Catherine's home town in the southern stretches of County Kildare. It's near where my father was born and raised, in Timahoe, near Stradbally, County Laois, and I can picture the flat green fields and mysterious fairy forts on wooded hills. She tells me what it was like growing up in an Athy pub and how she came to Australia with Louise, on their travels.

Catherine has been in Melbourne for a while and it's interesting to hear her views on Australian men and mores, giving a female slant to living here. She says the thing that strikes her most about Australians, compared with folk back home, is the relaxed, informal or casual nature they have. She cites the time she gave dinner to a couple of Australians, who had various complex dietary requirements—she went to a fair bit of trouble, thinking about the menu, shopping, cooking, and presenting the meal with care. The guests responded at the end with not much more than a 'thanks for supper', and Catherine felt a bit miffed, until she realised that if she had given them baked beans on toast they would have expressed their gratitude in exactly the same fashion. The 'no worries' ethos works both ways. Brought up to be effusive with my Ps and Qs, I think it might be rather a relief not to have to worry about them so much. Someone picks up your dropped hankie for you: 'Thanks, mate.' 'No worries.' Someone rescues you from drowning in the sea: 'Thanks, mate.' 'No worries.'

Time flies as we sort out the world—to the extent that when Catherine suddenly glances at her watch, she lets out a yelp. Late for work! She shoots out the door. But not before thanking me profusely. Old habits die hard.

> In Melbourne
> soft phrases of an Irish voice—
> mist.

Bloomsday

Saturday. My last Saturday in Melbourne! Only five full days left here, and I still haven't done any sightseeing. When I mentioned that to Kevin, he said he would take me on a grand tour of the city, and today is the day.

I tram it into town and walk to St Patrick's, the largest cathedral in Australia, where I'm due to meet Kevin. It's a vast basilica, alright, full of Mediterranean-Catholic mystery, or gloom if you prefer. I spot a stand of tiny burning candles and light one for my old schoolmate Jonesy, who is languishing in far-off Chichester, and Kevin's mum. I turn round and Kevin is right behind me, as if I've materialised him.

We stroll around the interior and notice that all the altars and statues of the Madonna have been covered up in purple cloth, waiting to be revealed on Easter Sunday. I'm struck by the disparity between Christian festivals and Australian seasons. The moment of resurrection, substantiated in Europe by buds and daffodils springing up, is in Australia subverted by the gravity of falling leaves.

Kevin tells me that his old Jesuit school used to be next door to the cathedral; he would come here with the school choir and remembers the master shouting at him: 'You, boy, do not sing!' He also remembers going up to the vertiginous bell tower as part of a school tour and opening a door, then suddenly being on the roof and the whole of Melbourne stretching giddily away down below; but he still had the presence of mind to scratch his name on a roof slate. It will be there till the end of time.

Lighting a church candle:
another prayer
going up in flames?

We leave St Pat's and walk to Flinders Street Station, the old Victorian railway hub, a gem of golden sandstone; its entrance facade displays eight small clocks that show the times of different train departures on thirteen different suburban lines. It's still the main rendezvous location in Melbourne: 'Will we meet under the clocks?' 'The clocks it is!'

Next on the sightseeing list is the Anglican cathedral, St Paul's, similar in shape to St Patrick's, but a bit smaller and jostled by skyscrapers; the interior has a brighter, more rational and clean-cut feel to it. I recall Krishnamurti's story of how the devil and a friend of his were walking down a road, when they saw a man pick up something from the ground and put it in his pocket. The friend said to the devil, 'What do you think he picked up?' 'A piece of Truth,' the devil replied. 'That's not going to be good for you,' said the friend. 'Oh, I wouldn't say that,' said the devil. 'I'm going to help him organise it.' Despite all that, I'm glad the Anglicans have let women become priests—a plaque on the wall marks the first ordination of a woman priest in 1995.

On Melbourne's rocks
God's First Fleet—
two cathedrals, beached.

We leave St Paul's, cross the road, and go into a Melbourne institution, the 'Collected Works' poetry bookshop,[*] run by an Aussified, but far from ossified, Briton called Kris Hemensley, and his wife Rita. It's a sprawling old shelf-lined shop, comprising one big room, and Seamus Heaney's mellow voice greets us on tape as we enter.

An old friend of Kevin, Kris is delighted to see us and proffers

---

[*] Collected Works Bookshop was Australia's only specialist commercial poetry bookshop. It closed end of November 2018.

a celebratory nip of whisky in small plastic cups. We toast poetry, take photos, swap poetry gossip. I find myself telling them about a famous Irish poet who was reading at a local festival—afterwards in a bar, a star-struck secondary school teacher went up to him with a gaggle of his sixth-form students, who were studying Gerard Manly Hopkins for their exams. The teacher, hoping for some nugget of inspiration from the famous poet, asked him to say a few words about Hopkins. The students leaned in, waiting to catch every word of the poet's insights. The poet took a leisurely sup of his Guinness, looked thoughtful, and then turning to his rapt audience, said: 'Hopkins needed a good wank!' The students couldn't believe their luck, the teacher collapsed in embarrassment. The poet followed it up with a contemptuous: 'Sprung rhythm—ha!'

Whisky-tipsy, gossip-wiser, we leave, ready for lunch. Kevin is not sure where to eat, so he phones his daughter Sophie, who is a reviewer of Melbourne restaurants. He tells her our requirements, including location, menu, price, and she comes up with the answer straightaway. Wouldn't that be a good job for someone? A restaurant consultant on the end of a phone.

We head south through sunshine as well as an idling Saturday crowd of tourists and shoppers, and emerge from side streets to a grand prospect of the Yarra River. It is broad, fast-flowing and flanked by huge apartment blocks, with something of the Thames or Seine about it. We find our designated riverside café, which is trendy and packed with mostly young people sitting outside having snacks and beers, shouting above the loud music. I'm not sure whether Sophie has matched us up with the right place, until we find a lovely tucked-away corner and can gaze at the Yarra.

We talk about the psychology of jokes and Kevin tells me his favourite gag, which is about a deaf old man being invited up on a stage and asked about his sex life and … well, the punchline revolves around him mistaking the word 'ghost' for 'goat'.

It feels seductive sitting beside the river and watching life strolling by. Melbourne has been consistently seductive—it regularly tops the charts as the most attractive city in the world—with its reliable sunshine, cafés, tree-lined streets, outgoing charm, smiles, friendliness, and no worries. Yet, as Jung always pointed out, there's a shadow side to everyone and everything; the brighter the light, the darker the shadow. The revered 'saintly' public man whose wife has borne the brunt of his private rages. At school the untouchable heroes were the rugger boys, haloed in light; but at the other end of the scale of our cult of physical prowess were the cleaners, local men with learning and physical disabilities, who were, at best, a caste of invisibles.

> A black elder inches
> across the highway lanes:
> walking frame a shopping trolley
> empty.

We leave the company of immortal youthful diners and proceed to Melbourne's famous winding lanes, where the walls are covered with graffiti artists' work.

The area is unexpectedly urban and gritty, as if we've struck a seam of flint while mining gold-bearing rocks; the sun is more or less obliterated in the narrow streets; huge elaborate murals lour from the sides of buildings; there's a famous guitarist with devil's horns; an Indigenous Australian giant, several storeys high, bearing an uprooted tree; a stencil-like portrait of Bob Marley with a quote next to it: 'You say you love rain, but you use an umbrella to walk under it.'

Yet for all our descent into a realm of fire-escapes, backdoors to nightclubs and scatterings of broken glass, we're not exactly in rats' alley where the dead men lose their bones; it's more a place where jokey local guides, dressed in bright blazers, lead guided tours of curious Japanese tourists.

> Aerosoled graffiti:
> artists spraying
> like cats.

Not yet satiated with visual art, we trek up the road to Federation Square and the National Gallery of Victoria (NGV) with its exhibition of Indigenous fabrics, baskets, hanging mobiles, and huge paintings. Soon my eyes are pixilated with coloured dots, as if the artists have deconstructed the world into particles, a pointillist vision of matter in which the atoms start moving around on the canvas as soon as you let down your conscious guard and swim into their kinetic reality.

By contrast, the white Australian art on the floor below constructs worlds of familiar, manageable forests and woodlands, glades filled with light, slender eucalyptus trees, pioneers taming the land. I'm drawn to the landscapes of John Glover, the artist whose work I saw in the Potter Museum. A favourite of mine is his 1840 painting, 'Patterdale Farm', Glover's own homestead in Mills Plains, northern Tasmania. Charles Harpur would have been twenty-seven at this time, and the painting makes me think of his own isolated farm in Eurobodalla, where he succumbed to TB. Glover's house is dwarfed by the interlocking, bush-tufted hills looming up behind it; the presence of cows and a lone man sitting against a eucalyptus, all picturesquely positioned, only emphasises the vast sky and sweep of land.

> ... beginningless
> endlessness
> of dot paintings ...

We are beginning to flag! Kevin, bless him, has long anticipated this and has planned for us to visit another Melbourne institution— one, astonishingly, he has never been to before: the Madame Brussels Cocktail Bar, which is named after a famous madame of the late 1800s, a certain Prussian-born woman named Caroline Lohman, who married an Englishman named Studholme Hodgson and made Melbourne her home. When money became tight in their adopted city, Caroline began managing a boarding house, before realising that more money was to be had from the second-oldest profession in the world. She gave herself the monicker, Madame Brussels, and flourished until a crackdown on the sex trade in the early 1900s.

The modern establishment is now lodged at the top of a tower block and has an awning-covered rooftop terrace. We emerge from the silent grey lift into the shrieks and squawks of the bar's ante-room, which is packed with groups of gaudily dressed women, faces daubed with blusher and lipstick the colour of red geraniums, con-vulsing with laughter. I've never seen so many people enjoying themselves so much; it's like the convergence of several hen parties, except all the women seem to be in their fifties. The waiters play to the gallery, dressed in high-camp pink blazers and shorts and sport-ing slick Gatsby-style brilliantined hair.

Two sparrows gate-crashing the Parrots' Ball, Kevin and I slip upstairs to the next level and manage to bag two bar stools at the edge of the terrace, with steepling views down to the street. We scan the menu and realise neither of us has ever had a proper cocktail before; the names are meaningless, and the ingredients sound like chemical formulae. I have no idea what a Moscow Mule ('vodka, lime, mint, laced with ginger beer and aromatic bitters') will taste like, nor the 'Love Juice' ('Bacardi Carta Blanca, berries, apple juice topped with bubbles'). Rather feebly, I go for a Bloody Mary. Kevin chooses a Manhattan. We must be Madame B's squarest-ever cus-tomers. I insist on a photo to mark this historic occasion and take out my camera. Before I can say 'Say cheese!', a mature, bosomy, retro-looking glamour puss confiscates the camera and says, 'I'll take one of you two boys'. Yes, it's Madame Brussels herself! Or at least her most recent incarnation, patrolling the floors to make sure everyone's having a good time.

And we are having a good time, to the extent that we suddenly realise time has gone belly up and we are going to be late for supper. We had arranged to meet others at an Italian restaurant in Lygon Street, as a sort of a premature farewell-to-Melbourne party for me. John, the blind literary editor; Pete R, the musician-lawyer who had played at the Irish bar, and his wife Polly; Catherine, my new Irish friend, will be there. We are also hoping to be joined by Penelope Buckley, the widow of Vincent Buckley. By a neat coincidence, Constant the medieval historian knows her and gave me her email address. I mailed her, inviting her to supper, anxious to meet the woman behind the man behind the award.

We dash from Madame Brussels as if we're escaping the clutches of the Mob. We catch a tram northwards and arrive at the restaurant, pink-faced from downed-in-one cocktails and running too fast. Pete and Polly are already there, chatting to Catherine. We settle down in the corner, feeling quite squashed in, and distribute menus; then John arrives and is escorted to the table by a waiter. We leap up, guide John to his seat, and re-assemble ourselves. A few minutes later Penelope Buckley arrives, and, well-rehearsed, we leap up and squeeze her in to the table too. I was told by Strazz the Teacher that Penelope was considered a great beauty at university and I can see straightaway the truth of this in her face and bright, charming manner. I'm keen to talk to her, but the room is noisy and the acoustics unhelpful, every sound bouncing off the walls and tiled floor and gargling in our ears. Also, I'm feeling quite tipsy from my huge Bloody Mary, and the action-packed day is taking its toll. So when Kevin suggests, after the main course, that we might adjourn to his house, it sounds perfect.

We pile into two cars, me and Kevin and Catherine driven by Penelope. At one set of traffic lights, Penelope exclaims, 'Oh, I so love traffic lights, I love their colours; I hope they never change them.' It's the first time I've considered traffic lights for their aesthetic appeal and not as objects of irritation or anxiety. It's a small consciousness-raising moment.

> Traffic lights at night:
> three new planets
> swimming into my ken.

At Kevin's house it's an enormous relief to sprawl on the sofa and talk without craning an ear to scoop up the murmurings of a reply.

As I'm daydreaming about being in the middle of an Australian Bloomsday, I'm importuned to read a couple of my poems, not something I'm wont to do in front of small groups of intimates, but I give it a lash. Then Pete sings us a few songs, finger-picking away on his guitar. He introduces one of the songs by saying that his daughter had asked him to write it for her twenty-first birthday and sing it at her party. He'd been reluctant—'Aw, you don't want your old dad embarrassing you in front of your mates'—but she'd been insistent. The birthday party was raucous, a full-blooded disco, young things dancing like Maenads, and Pete had thought, 'Nah. It's not going to work'. But silence was called for and he performed the song to a hushed and reverent audience; apparently not a dry eye in the huge tent.

We wait with bated breath and he launches into this song; its wistful lyrics and minor chords give us all trembling lips.

By now, the supper in the restaurant seems like yesterday, Madame Brussels like a strange dream I've had, and lighting a candle in St Patrick's a childhood memory.

Penelope volunteers to drive me home and, on the way, offers to take me out for a drive on Tuesday. A car and driver at my disposal, she says. It seems an imposition and I demur, but she's insistent: anywhere I want. I thank her and tell her I shall think on it.

Trusty old Sappho is too sleepy to meow guilt into me. I barely reach the bed before I'm away in the dreaming.

> Late night: friends and music,
> fresh figs and coffee;
> how long can a sofa stretch?

Heide high

It's Sunday morning and I'm still saturated with the day before: sitting in the café beside the Yarra with Kevin and watching life flow past; gazing at huge graffiti murals; rubbing shoulders with Madame Brussels; listening to Pete singing …

I'm now counting down my days in Melbourne with multiplying tinges of sadness. Yesterday was so full, I feel I could lie in my bed till I leave the city and simply replay the day's happenings.

Tea and toast bring me back to the ship of the present and I can hear the look-out at the top of the mast shouting, 'Full day ahead!'

I walk to the Thresherman's Bakehouse at exactly the same time and on the same route and in the same warm sunny weather as last week. Constant and Maryna and their friends are camped inside the café and I join them on the long table. They include a retired university teacher who has recently taken up medieval Irish for the fun of it; an art historian whose husband, a retired Harvard-educated teacher, had come to hear me read at the Irish bar; a man who lived in Booterstown in Dublin for twenty-three years. It's a rare experience to hear a table of people speak unselfconsciously about literature, music, Latin, Greek, archaeology, medieval history, poetry, and Ireland, all things dear to me. The clichés back home about Australia being a cultural desert seem to have little basis. In Melbourne I haven't been able to escape culture, from art to poetry to music to second-hand guitar shops and book shops. Once back in Cork I'll need to camp out in a concrete underground car park for a week to get all this culture out of me.

*

After lunch, Maryna, Constant and I set off to Heide, an art museum situated outside the city on land that belonged to a bohemian couple called John and Sunday Reed. They were art lovers and patrons who turned their country home (called Heide House) into a commune of painters and poets in the 1930s and '40s, like the Bloomsbury group—complete with the obligatory ménage à trois, involving the two Reeds and Sidney Nolan.

We arrive early afternoon. The old house is set in rolling parkland, Australian-style, with gum trees rising from patchy yellowy grass. We proceed, gently, through three distinct museum spaces in the old house and its annexes. Sidney Nolan and Albert Tucker are two of the featured artists, as well as Charles Blackman.

Blackman's 'schoolgirl series' fills two large rooms. His girls are more often than not standing in post-apocalyptic cityscapes, with empty streets, sharp angles and ominous shadows. As though living in a perpetual summer, they wear broad-brimmed straw hats, with their faces in shadow, as if they are wearing masks. Sometimes the artist accentuates the eyes, making the pupils look exaggeratedly downwards or sideways, conveying surprise or fear at some terrible thought or something beyond the frame of the painting.

I can't make up my mind about the paintings. The figures' two-dimensional, stick-limbed quality is a reminder that Blackman was an illustrator on a newspaper in his early days; the settings rehearse the urban alienation trope a bit too easily. And yet they do evoke childhood states of innocence, isolation, suspicion, vulnerability, loneliness and a sense of a big bad adult world 'out there'. After two rooms of the images, my mood was altered.

We have a cup of tea in the outdoor café, during which Constant entertains us by thinking out aloud about his imminent lecture on Zoroastrianism. It prompts me to mention the time when I once had to write about Zoroastrian death and funeral rituals for a book. I wanted to give an example of a modern Zoroastrian funeral to show the continuity with the ancient culture, and preferably that of someone well known. How many famous Zoroastrians did I know? Nada. As the deadline became critical, I remember I was on a train and looking surreptitiously at someone's newspaper. The pop singer Freddie Mercury had just died—his face was splashed on an inside double-spread, and the caption said: 'Zoroastrian funeral for Mercury.' I nearly sang, 'We are the Champions'.

After tea, and with words like Ahura Mazda echoing in my mind, we stroll around the grounds, relieved to escape Blackman's empty streets. I'm still not used to seeing flocks of white cockatoos in trees, and it's strange to stumble on the mighty Yarra River in a much-reduced, humble form, slinking through bushy land at the back of the grounds like a long sludge-textured crocodile.

Maryna drives us back and drops me off in Fitzroy. We exchange farewells, and they tell me they might be coming to Ireland in the summer. I immediately start daydreaming about the holy wells and medieval ruins I can take them to.

At home, Sappho unleashes a volley of meows, as if she thought I'd abandoned her for good. 'How could I!' I reply. I give her a cuddle and look at emails. Kevin says that despite his mum's worrying condition, he is still going to fly to Sydney tomorrow, to attend a university seminar. Penelope's email repeats her offer to take me out on Tuesday. Kevin and others have recommended either St Kilda, Melbourne's seaside resort, or the Healesville Animal Sanctuary, about forty minutes or so beyond the city limits. I reply to Penelope to say I'd like to go to Healesville. I haven't yet seen the full panoply of Australian wildlife, and I can't go home without reporting that I've played poker with a koala, swum with a platypus, or tickled a dingbat.

> Cockatoos in branches;
> summer snowflakes falling
> upwards.

St Kilda

Monday. With Tuesday and Healesville sorted out, I decide to go to St Kilda to investigate its reputation as a picturesque, bohemian and seedy seaside resort. With the sky clear blue and the temperature a perfect 22 degrees, I hop on the marvellous 69 tram, which takes me south of the Yarra all around the houses, industrial estates, and past a local cricket ground that seems to go on forever.

We arrive in the heart of St Kilda in Acland Street, which is pedestrianised and crowded. The buildings are small, low rise, and a mixture of tourist and practical shops and cafés. Foremost of the latter is Monarch, an eastern European cake shop with old sepia photos on the walls, and casually strewn books and memorabilia. I eke out a vanilla slice with coffee then saunter down Acland and join a big thoroughfare, Fitzroy Street, not so much boho as seedy or desolate, with a string of burger joints and fruit-machine parlours, mostly empty. It has a modern Wild West feel to it, so I keep going and dive into a side road, where I see a small barber's shop and a youngish couple sitting outside on next door's doorstep, chatting and smoking cigarettes in the sunshine. I have been meaning to have a haircut for days, but haven't had the pluck to do so in Fitzroy.

The barber's place is empty and I ask the couple if it's closed; they turn out to be the hairdressers themselves, and the man leaps up and guides me in. He is from Macedonia, in his thirties, with very few words of English. His board of listed cuts includes a 'flat top', which sounds like a coffee, and a 'Mohawk', but there's nothing that says 'gentle trim of hair and beard, please'. I realise my haircut could go horribly wrong. I think up the best English words and supplement them by making my fingers do a delicate snipping motion to indicate my requirements, and we settle down in happy silence.

> Word-snipped Macedonian barber:
> an open drawer—
> a cutthroat, gleaming.

I leave like a shorn Samson—neat and trim but suddenly weak and hungry. I could murder a Philistine, but will accept a cheese sandwich.

I keep walking along hot metalled roads and arrive at Barkly Street, another thoroughfare roaring with traffic, and spot an un-obtrusive café, calling itself a bakery, with a bench or two outside on the pavement beside the torrent of cars. It looks like a forbidding roadside shack, but hunger forces me inside. I expect to see Ned Kelly and his gang look round with thousand-yard stares, but it's small and cosy, with, as usual, smiling young women with their hair piled up and diamond nose studs. Through a hatch you can see big ovens producing all sorts of fancy breads. The music being played is 'Smokestack Lightning' by Howlin' Wolf, a favourite of mine. I take this as a sign from the gods and stay, eating outside, sitting on the corner, watching all the cars go by.

After lunch, I realise I haven't seen St Kilda's beach or the sea yet. Before I left the northern hemisphere, all talk was of me swimming in the ocean and being eaten by a shark or stung to death by jellyfish or being picked up as a refugee and stuck in an internment camp. It's strange how many scary anecdotes people have about Australia— people who have never been there. Friend-of-a-friend stories, which always begin with, 'Apparently …' People love Australia being a big bad dangerous place. In Europe, where it's almost impossible to die at the jaws or a sting of a wild creature, Australia fulfils the func-tion of a mythic Hades, an underworld stuffed with monsters and tortures.

So, the sea it is. I pass Luna Park, where a giant infernal machine equipped with carriages is whisking passengers into the sky, then jerking them around and tipping them over. The idea, pure and simple, is to make them feel they are going to die. And it's working, to judge by the blood-curdling screams of children.

I emerge from the streets onto a boulevard of palm trees and a beautiful sandy beach adorned with a few sunbathers. Even the sea is calm, lapping gently at the sand; on a small promontory in the distance a thin white lighthouse rises like a minaret; it's hard to imagine a shark in a hundred miles. Tempting though it is to lie down and snooze in the sun, I know that if I do I will never get up again, and you can snooze on a beach anywhere, but I might not return to St Kilda again.

With a puritan's sigh, I continue on my way along the promenade, consisting of private houses, with no amusement arcade in sight. I arrive back at Acland Street and catch a tram for the centre of Melbourne. I want to see the main National Gallery of Victoria before I leave.

> St Kilda's ocean;
> the lighthouse keeps blinking—
> astonished at infinity.

The NGV is a huge modern building, and its wide glass-fronted façade has a thin, evenly-spread waterfall pouring down across it like liquid glass.

Inside I see an exhibition called 'Love and Emotion', with paintings and books from different ages, loosely related to love. I think it's impossible to write poems about love, or to paint it, because it's too interior and intimate to be expressed, except in the feeblest, or overcompensatory dramatic, terms. Still, I'm curious and it's worth going to, if only for a painting by Henry Fuseli of a young John Milton sleeping under a tree and the apocryphal story the caption relates.

The young Milton, taking time off from studies at Cambridge, falls asleep under a tree; while he is slumbering, a young woman appears and leaves him a note on which are lines of an Italian verse. Milton wakes up and discovers the note, but not the woman, and is inspired to go to Italy. He will claim to his dying days that the woman and her verse caused him to write Paradise Lost. That's the story, an allegory of the workings of the Muse. In fact, the Muse that Milton actually names in his epic poem is the rather masculine or gender-neutral Holy Spirit, not the sensuous swan-necked beauty Fuseli has created. Dr Johnson was scornful of Milton's 'Turkish contempt for females'; but his life was dominated by them, three wives, three living daughters, on whom the blind old poet became increasingly dependent.

Back home, Sappho, my furry Muse, is in her basket and doesn't come out to meow at me. I wonder if she senses I'm leaving soon.

Healesville

Tuesday, the day before the day before I leave. When a place is so far away from home that it casts doubt on the likelihood of one's return, it concentrates the mind wonderfully. I wish Dr Johnson had written that.

Penelope arrives at noon and we set off eastward along dual carriageways, headed for Warburton, about fifty miles away. We chat amiably about poetry, Australia, Ireland and how she met Vincent Buckley. She was a young slip of a girl at university, and he a charismatic poet and lecturer. I think of the Muse and Milton and his Italian lady.

As we delve deeper into our lives, we discover various parallels and coincidences. My ears prick up when she uses the word 'iconodules' (icon lovers) unselfconsciously, and I have to tell her that iconoclasm is one of my pet subjects; she then tells me that she's joined a Byzantine Greek reading group in the city; which leads me to say that I studied Greek at university for a short while before changing to English literature; she can't believe that, because she, too, studied Classics, at Melbourne, and also quickly changed to English. She then mentions writing about the Third Crusade—a period I happen to know about because I've written about the Crusades myself; and so it goes on, as if we've lived each other's lives on different continents, at different times, and with different people.

Our conversation is so engrossing that I don't fully concentrate on the countryside, the first I've seen of Australia. But I see enough to appreciate the Yarra River valley, rolling hills, stands of eucalyptus, creeks and billabongs, and the odd vineyard. I had imagined the land just beyond Melbourne to be parched flat outback and it's a surprise to see such a fecund, undulating and varied landscape. It could be the south of France, except for a flock of cockatoos above a tree or a wallaby poking through a bush.

Our aim is to turn left to Healesville at some point, but, caught in a sunny web of chattering, we miss it and sail on along an increasingly empty road through green hills. After a while I begin to get more anxious and puzzled. We haven't passed or been passed by a car for quite some time; road signs have petered out. I say to Penelope, 'Have you seen the film *Deliverance*?' Luckily she hasn't.

Eventually we come to a grassy lay-by in a sort of forest glade; there's a tourist map displayed in a glass-fronted wooden frame. We stop and peruse it and see where we went wrong.

By the time we reach Healesville it's three o'clock, and we're both starving. We sit in the outdoor café, under awnings, and peck at our sandwiches, rather like the ibis who pokes around us pecking up our crumbs. I see something rodenty under a table, but somehow it seems part of the habitat; nobody shrieks or stands on a chair.

> Outdoor café—
> black rat beneath a table!—
> a plague on it!

We hit the sanctuary trail, which winds through various habitats where the animals lounge around, like hosts too drunk to rise to their feet when the guests come to visit.

I suddenly feel excited. It's one thing seeing a koala bear on a stamp or postcard—but there it is, the actual creature, hugging a small gum tree. It is so still that we both wonder whether it's a soft toy, put there to encourage the real koalas to interact. Then I spy the twitch of an ear. I have never seen an animal look so much like the soft toy of itself.

We follow the path to an enclosure where a group of small kangaroos is sunbathing on the grass, some propped up on their elbows and staring at the world in an uncannily human way. Their L-shaped legs look as if they could be folded up like a deckchair.

We then pass a solitary emu, obscured by bushes, and arrive at the duck-billed platypus 'aquarium', all dimly lit and filled with rockeries and weeds. I had imagined platypuses to be quite large, like small seals, but the one we see is only about a foot long, a dear little thing, swimming round and round a rock as if chasing its watery shadow.

Farther on is the Tasmanian devil. I'm expecting a tree-leaping, prehensile monkey-cum-bear-cum-snake, a manticore of a creature; instead it's a small, black, pig-like creature, half hopping and half stumbling around its enclosure. It looks rather cute. Its demonic tag apparently comes from its horrendous screech, as well as power-ful jaws and a ferocious appetite. Sweet little piggy is actually the Rottweiler of marsupials.

The next enclosure of rocks and shrubs seems empty. Then look-ing directly down we see the sheeny brown fur of a wombat, curled up asleep. We stare into its back, willing it to move and perform; but the creature is in the wombat land of Nod, dreaming of digging a huge hole in the MCG cricket pitch.

We drive back to the city, satiated with animals and still full of conversation, but this time concentrating on not missing any turns. Penelope shows me her home, a haven of paintings, books, and memories of Vincent. The sun is setting in the huge tree in the back garden, which has the feel of an Australian Eden. It's difficult to tear myself away, but I can sense Sappho waiting for her supper. I hadn't planned to be out this late in the evening. For almost three weeks I've been neurotically worried that she might keel over during my watch, and I'm determined that no mishaps should occur just before I depart for good.

Penelope drives me home and invites me to join her Byzantine reading group for supper on the morrow. Another thing I would never have imagined back home: supper with Australian Byzantists in an Italian restaurant.

Sappho is indeed waiting for her supper. She looks so normal compared with the creatures I've just seen. Not an assemblage of parts, like the platypus or Tasmanian devil, but pure, uncomplicated, non-marsupial catypuss.

Missing a turning on the road
but every signpost
says 'Home'.

Walking to Byzantium

Wednesday. My last full day, the day of gooey goodbyes. Kevin is still in Sydney, arriving back this evening, and he will call round tomorrow morning on his way to work to say his last adieu.

First up is Catherine of Kildare, whom I meet at the Thresherman's Bakehouse, now a familiar haunt. It's pleasantly sunny—of course it is!—still no sign of proper autumn—and we sit at a pavement table. It must be the hundredth time I've sat in a café in warm sunshine. How will I re-adapt to the mizzle and mist of Cork? It's a brief hello and farewell, since Catherine has to go off to teach her Colombian women. We take stock, take a photo, then stroll down the street to Catherine's tram stop and exchange warm wishes, rejoining our paths to unknown lives ahead.

I then hurry to the Victorian splendour of Graduate House in the university campus. It's where I was originally going to reside before the Sappho-sitting opportunity came up, and I've been invited to lunch there by the principal. From her personalised invitation I am assuming it will be a low-key twosome, a bite to eat and some desultory chit-chat.

It turns out to be a formal luncheon for a hundred people, all dressed formally! The event also includes a presentation by a nurse named Diana about her work in Tanzania. Taken aback, I splutter apologies to everyone I meet about my dress—open shirt, and trousers closer to jeans than anything else—but thankfully the 'no worries' approach to life comes into its own.

Ten tables of ten VIP-looking people fill the elegant room. I am given a name badge and positioned between two women in their mid- to late-twenties, Sara, on my right, and Bettina on my left. It soon transpires that everyone seems to have a connection with Tanzania, or is involved in social or medical work, or education, or international relations. Except me. Nevertheless, the principal introduces me to the room as a visiting poet; she repeats what I've just told her—that I was expecting a cosy tête-à-tête—and everyone has a good old laugh. I suspect I'm supposed to stand up and take a small bow, but I'm too unconfident about my trousers. I keep my head down and engage my two companions in conversation while trying to spear my slippery pasta. Both women turn out to be high-powered movers and shakers in economics and international relations, and both are curious to know what I'm doing in Melbourne. I'm halfway through an extended reply when there's the clinking of a glass, hushing, and the principal introduces the guest speaker.

Diana starts her talk, with the help of a slideshow. Images of destitute Tanzanian villagers appear on the wall, and our half-finished, first-world dishes suddenly feel out of place. She is fluent and persuasive, describing the Tanzanian village she is working in and the problems of raising money for a small school and rudimentary healthcare. What she and her colleagues have achieved on a shoestring seems like a miracle. Poets are always agonising about their 'usefulness' to the world, and people like Diana make that introspection more acute.

Afterwards there are questions, and I'm expecting a round of 'Well done, you!' But the first questioner, an elderly gent, bowls an aggressive bouncer at her, or perhaps it's just the Australian way of straight speaking? 'Aw, look, what you say is all very well, but why don't you focus more on birth control information?' Diana fields it adroitly, but other questions induce a forward defensive rather than hooks to the boundary.

As the questions tail off, I'm aware that I'm due to meet Amanda and Denise at the university to say goodbye, so I slip off as soon as the lecture finishes.

Conveniently, I find Amanda and Denise chatting together in Amanda's office. I don't linger, dispensing small mementoes of a Connemara bracelet and Irish fudge. Old Irish proverb: 'Fudge speaks louder than words.' Smiles, handshakes, hugs all round. I leave with another pang of satisfaction and sadness.

Back home I continue bits of tidying and hoovering while Sappho follows me around meowing for something I can't guess at; or perhaps her arthritis is giving her pain and she just wants to share it with me?

After dark I set out again to meet Penelope and her Byzantine group at an Italian restaurant. I arrive at the appointed place, but there's no one there and I fear I don't have the right venue. And I've left my phone behind. So I sit on a bench on the other side of the road, and wait to see if anyone turns up. Behind me is a tree-filled park, swathed in darkness, where I've been told the eyes of possums glow from the tree branches at night. I don't have to turn round; I can see them.

Eventually I spy Penelope arriving at the restaurant opposite, clearly looking for me. I hail her and she leads me up the road to the correct pizza joint.

The array of Byzantists who greet me are reminiscent of Constant's post-mass Bakehouse group, consisting of about a dozen men and women, mostly retired. I sit next to the team leader, Roger, who is a former professor, avuncular and erudite. The last time I studied Greek seriously was at school, and it was just me doing it. I had endless classes with a master nicknamed 'Neggers', just me and him, no escape. I don't know who was more gloomy, me, trying to figure out Homeric optatives under extreme pressure, or him, wondering what his Oxford First had amounted to. In fairness, we got on fine most days; but two years stuck together in a classroom designed for thirty boys …

Our discussion about iconoclasm and my own attempt at translating the Lysistrata takes a back seat when the woman opposite starts recounting when she saw the Beatles in Melbourne back in the sixties. Her expressions become those of the young teenager she once was as she tells us how she and her two friends joined the crowds outside the Beatles' hotel, waiting for an appearance at the window—then wild screaming at a glimpse of Ringo. Sometime after the Beatles left town, the three girls went to the hotel and got a sympathetic chambermaid to sneak them upstairs and into the room the Beatles stayed in. They walked around the holy shrine in a daze, touching items of furniture. Icons!

After supper, Penelope drives me home and we bid each other farewell. Another moment of tristesse.

Because it's our last night, I let Sappho curl up on my lap like a furry slug.

> Watching the pizzas arrive
> the eyes of Byzantists—
> golden tesserae!

Fare forward, not farewell

Thursday. This is it! Last hours in Melbourne. I feel wistful. I might not ever return.

As promised, Kevin drops round for breakfast, bringing almond croissants in his saddle bag. As it happens I've just been out round the corner and bought … almond croissants, so I instruct Kevin to take his away.

It's hard to know how to sum up and bring closure to three intense weeks, and for me to express my deep gratitude for all he's done. Perhaps a 'Thanks, mate', 'No worries', will do it?

We ease into our coda, him talking me through his trip to Sydney, sitting in an arts meeting in which he is the only man among ten women. Reversalising the masculine hegemony, perhaps, to use seminar-speak?

His mum continues to be poorly, and I can see the cloud over his head remains.

Then it's time to part.

> Goodbye hug—
> words and words and words
> holding their tongues.

I watch Kevin cycle off from the house for a final time and hope that his mum pulls through.

Last preparations. Wiping surfaces, heaping up Sappho's bowl with her pellets. I've ordered a taxi for 11.45 am. It seems like plenty of

time, but it soon races away. I go out to the backyard for one last time
and there's Sappho, sitting in the sunshine.

> Insouciant puss,
> pretending you won't miss me;
> eyes blurry.

When the taxi comes the driver turns out to be a cheery Australian-
Pakistani who snaps me out of my elegiac mood. I'm bursting to
tell him about my weeks in Melbourne, but he gets in first and tells
me his life story. The bit that surprises me most is his father being
in the Pakistan navy and fighting in two wars against India. I can
remember various Kashmir skirmishes but not two wars, which is
disconcerting. He adds that Pakistanis and Indians get on very well
in Melbourne.

We arrive at the airport far too early, but I'm mindful of my
Singapore experience when I nearly missed the plane and keep
checking my watch.

The flight will only take an hour, a short hop of a large kangaroo.

Till now I haven't allowed myself to think about Sydney at all.
When I planned the trip I always knew I wanted to spend some
time there, to see two old university friends, Sarah and Marian, and
pursue the trail of my putative relative, Charles Harpur.

For three weeks Sydney has shimmered at the back of my mind
without fully intruding.

> Leaving Melbourne:
> Brunswick, Fitzroy, Carlton, Richmond—
> Ah, the old world.

Sydney

Touch down! Security. Passport. Baggage reclaim. Airport arrivals are never designed to make you feel welcome.

I make my way to a pick-up point outside the terminal, as previously indicated by Sarah, and stand with a dozen other travellers in what looks like an underground car park. Cars enter and circle us like bored sharks, then reverse into spaces. People get out and the waiting travellers diminish in number. It reminds me of waiting to be picked up at boarding school, when my mum was always the last to arrive.

I sit on a bench and bide my time.

Eventually I hear a shout, 'Excuse me, are you James Harpur?' I turn round and I see Sarah staring at a dishevelled, crumpled, seedy old gent! Well, she hasn't seen me in years and I do now have a beard and a super-cool hat. I leap up and reveal myself to her with a jolly cry of 'Sarah!' and we have a hug. She looks the same as I remembered her years ago: tall, pretty, long brown hair, with a genteel crinkle about the eyes.

We drive back to her home in Annandale, and straightaway Sydney looks more undulating, complex and busier than Melbourne, where the long straight roads and trams seemed to simplify life.

Back home, Alexi, her son, answers the door. Last time I saw him he was nine years old and was being carsick on my carpet; now he is over six foot, handsome, suave and sociable: I almost want to be sick on his carpet.

That evening Marian arrives, also looking how I remembered her, with her trademark curly-crinkly hair now stylishly white; she wears a khaki, pleated dress and a scarf, and wastes no time filling me in on her life—marriage, family, moving house, the film business. Meanwhile Sarah and Alexi cook veggie fritters. With wine to aid the memory and loosen our feelings, we reminisce till we are pink in the face.

Marian was the first woman I met at university, at a party, her cheerful antipodean face a Sydney sunrise among the drizzly visages of convent girls, boarding school girls, day girls, almost all the girls—though 'all' hardly suggests the scarcity of girls. There was a rumour that boys outnumbered girls by nine to one, so every girl was seen from a straight male point of view as a precious specimen of a practically extinct species.

Marian seemed to be worldly and confident, and her room in her college annex, Wolfson Court, became an unofficial salon. She was the soul of calm and creativity when she produced two of my plays, short one-act dramas that were staged in college. The first was about computer dating and fate—can computerised personal details really match up people successfully? The other was about a Classics don who has an affair with a female student, and their situation parallels the story of Aeschylus's *Agamemnon*, the play they were studying. Although my plays were flawed, youthful first attempts at writing, Marian took them seriously and organised the sets, heaved furniture, distributed posters, whipped the lighting techs into shape, and so on. Now she does the equivalent as a high-powered film producer.

After energetic forays into the past, we all begin to feel our long days catch up with us. I creak upstairs to bed, picturing David and Yol, now back from New York, embracing their sweet querulous cat.

> Old friends!
> What have our lives lost
> to make memories so pleasant?

Harbour

Friday. I wake early and get ready for Marian to take me out to breakfast. Sarah has gone out to what she calls a 'boot-camp gym', which doesn't sound like the style of the laid-back Sarah I used to know.

Breakfast, I'm told, is something that Sydneyites go out to a lot; perhaps other Australians do as well. It feels counterintuitive. I like rolling out of bed and into the kitchen in slippers and pyjamas. Actually I could probably do that in an Australian café and no one would notice.

Marian arrives and we set off to a small corner place, a few streets away. The road is quiet, and opposite there's a small leafy square with a playground. The café is filled with young men and women, and I can't tell if they're on the way to work or just lolling around like us. We sit outside on the pavement and Marian orders a 'Scando', which is two boiled eggs, toast, an apricot and cheese. I have an elaborate toasted sandwich with haloumi, mushrooms and tomato.

We chat about this and that: life, death and the cosmos, where our lives are going, where they have been. When you haven't seen someone for a long time, and probably won't see them again for a long time, you punctuate current trivia with dramatic historical revelations in the tone of trivia—'Oh yes, he died several years ago—his wife moved back to Luxembourg and took up with a bald psychotherapist'.

Marian reveals that she has had to sell the old family home in central Sydney, a matter of great sadness. She will move out in a couple of days and is having a farewell party tomorrow night, to which I'm invited. I haven't been to a party in a long time, at least not the sort Marian throws—pink champagne, jazz music and a waiter or two, that sort of thing. Will my social skills bear the strain?

Back home, Sarah returns from her gym, precariously balanced between invigorated and knackered. Today she's suggested doing a waterborne tour of Sydney Harbour.

We drive through back streets to a jetty in Balmain, a leafy residential district of mature stylish houses bedded in on slopes. A chunky ferry boat arrives and whisks us off to Central Quay, the main ferry station. I had thought, innocently, that Sydney Harbour was really just a harbour, like Cork harbour or Liverpool, a decent-sized area for ships to dock. I had no idea it was a vast inlet around which a city of skyscrapers and waterside villas had sprung up.

> Sydney Harbour sea—
> the sun picking silver threads
> everywhere it looks.

We are skimming along the water and soon approach Sydney Harbour Bridge and the Opera House, as if we're sailing into tourist posters and will emerge at Uluru or the Great Barrier Reef.

At Central Quay we hop off, pause to watch an Indigenous busker sitting on the pavement playing a didgeridoo, then dash to catch a bigger ferry for Watson's Bay, which lies at the head of the inlet.

This new boat chugs along at a decent speed, passing facades of design-sculpted houses with palm trees sprouting around them.

At Watson's Bay, a small cove where the sea tamely laps the sand, we are completely removed from the density of the city. We embark on a soporific coastline walk, past villas and small beaches, rocks reserved for nude bathers, and end up at South Head. I have yet to spy a bronzed surfer!

Here we stand at the eastern edge of Australia, gazing out at the

South Pacific Ocean, a shiny mass of endless restlessness. I feel like Keats's stout Cortez. Fancy growing up next to the South Pacific! An 'ocean' is simply a classified stretch of water, yet I've always thought the words 'Pacific Ocean' had a ring of such immensity. Even the mighty Atlantic seemed parochial by comparison; and as for the Irish Sea, or English Channel …

I remember that Captain Cook sailed past this very South Head in 1770, preferring to weigh anchor at Botany Bay down the coast. It would be another eighteen years till Commodore Arthur Phillip and the eleven ships of the First Fleet, with their cargo of wretched male and female convicts, adults and children, arrived in what Phillip called 'the finest harbour in the world', in which 'a thousand sail of the line may ride in the most perfect security …' About 1,500 poor souls were at sea for 252 days, a journey that now takes just over 20 hours by plane.

In 1799 it was the turn of Joseph Harpur, convicted of being part of a robbery, to undergo this voyage. I imagine a young Charles later pestering him with questions such as: 'What was it like on the ship, Papa?'—just like me asking my dad what the war was like—and Papa giving a heavy sigh and changing the subject.

We stroll back along our path in diminishing sunshine, catch a crowded ferry back to Central Quay, and watch the sunset glancing off the glass of the Opera House.

> The footpath to the Pacific turns
> a corner—
> *thalatta, thalatta!*

Roots

Saturday: the Blue Mountains and the trail of the lonesome life of Charles Harpur, my putative ancestor, which began in the town of Windsor, about thirty miles away.

Sarah and I drive off mid-morning and negotiate early morning Sydney traffic, crossing the huge Anzac Bridge, then the Harbour Bridge, both of which rear up over the city in a rapturous way and staple it together.

We make our way through suburbs and out onto a dual carriage-way heading northwest towards Windsor. The countryside is green from recent rains and it's perfect weather yet again, sunny and 22 degrees.

At Windsor, Charles's birthplace, we park and look around for buildings dating from his era. Charles was born in 1813. From an early age he wanted to be a poet, and not just any old poet but the first poet of Australia, born and bred on its soil. To this end he settled for a life that would put his poetry first. He took a variety of jobs, including sorting letters in a post office, sheep farming, and latterly, being an assistant gold mining commissioner. He lived in and around Sydney for most of his life until the late 1850s when he moved to a farm at Eurobodalla in southeast New South Wales. All this time he was firing off hundreds of poems, letters and critical articles to newspapers. Not only did he gain a reputation as a learned and lyrical poet, but also as a campaigner. He was a fierce republican who spoke out against transportation. His poems could be witty and satirical, but his reputation rests on his lyrical descriptions of nature and its relationship to some divine power.

To give one example: in 'A Coastal View' he describes being alone on a cliff face, watching the sea and observing plants and creatures that, in their movement, energy and colour, are like small embodiments of the great life force itself. Against the base of the cliffs 'Beats the white wrath of the relentless surge' and on the rockface

> … a nameless shrub
> With flame-bright blossom, tufts each guttered ledge
> That holds a scanty soil; and rarer still,
> Green runners from some sheltering crevice throw
> Their tendrils o'er the shelves, and trailing thence
> Touch the stern faces of the rocks with beauty.

The lines have a lovely lilt to them—Wordsworth would have been purring. The poem is already full of life and movement—the sea, the green tendrils, fiery shrubs—but then Charles adds even more kinetic energy to the scene with birds and sea creatures:

> Below, the porpoise breaches, and the crab
> Waits for his prey …
>   … or, more remote,
> Out in the watery spaces may be seen
> Some solitary diver's shining back.
> Sea-gulls go clanging by, and overhead
> Sits the white-breasted hawk …

Charles struggled to gain the literary reputation that he yearned for during his lifetime. He was an honest, open, impulsive man, full of the certainty of his poetic vocation, yet he was wary of literary circles and metropolitan elites. Latterly, on his farm, he felt isolated and neglected. He lost his job in the gold mining business in 1866. The following year, his thirteen-year-old son killed himself accidentally with a shotgun. Charles took it badly. The same year there were terrible floods that washed away parts of his property. By this time he was suffering from tuberculosis, and he had a young family to support. The death of his young son and the floods finished him off. But his poetry has lived on. I wanted to tell him that, and eventually I penned these lines as a letter-poem:

> Dear Charles,
> I never got as far as Singleton,
> Jerry's Plains, or Eurobodalla,
> your farm above the banked lane
> of grassy verges and eucalyptus;
> your grave, and that of Charles, your son
> embedded by the farmhouse.
> *I did* see Windsor, and tried in vain
> to imagine you as a youngster
> from your sepia daguerrotype—
> like an old Confederate soldier,
> waterfall beard, greyish white,
> the baleful stare of Elijah.
> Nearby, your friend, the Hawkesbury,
> uncoiled through autumn fields;
> and Homer was whispering in the trees—
> my favourite lines were yours as well:
> *'The race of men is as the race of leaves:*
> *some the winds shed upon the ground,*
> *while still the fructifying boughs put others forth,*
> *to flourish in their season. So of men*
> *the generations die and are renewed.'*
>
> You wrote that after floods ruined
> your farm, the first flush of TB,
> and Charles's death had broken you.
> Then came your self-obituary:
> *'Here lies Charles Harpur,*
> *who at fifty years of age*
> *came to the conclusion,*

that he was living in a sham age,
under a sham Government,
and amongst sham friends,
and that any World whatever
must therefore be
a better world than theirs …'

I can hardly bear to think about
your purgatory before death,
the fading of your errant quest
to wrestle poetry from truth
in a brave new New South Wales
constructed by Old World gentry
and daily floggings; no wonder you'd sail
to the wine-dark plain of Troy
as you sorted letters in a post office
or spent those years farming sheep
to scrape the time to write, then face
ordeal by rejection slip.

What kept you going? Faith? Or fear
of meeting Milton in the afterlife?
Or the magical ingress of ideas
appearing like your ducks in flight
following the windings of the vale,
and still enlarging lengthwise, and in places too
oft breaking off into solitary dots.
Or were you rapt by your Muse's eyes—
two midnights of passionate thought—
igniting images in your mind,
such as your beach crab, who waits
for his prey amid the wave-washed stones
that glisten to the sun—gleaming himself
whenever he moves, as if his wetted shell
were breaking into flame.

Your parents brought you rootless
into a land of grog and marsupials.
Did you ever ask your father, Joseph,
about his childhood in Kinsale?
Or orientate yourself with stories
of family lore, like those I heard—
how, in the wake of Richard de Clare,
we Harpurs came to Wexford?
Or of your father's coffin-voyage
across the southern seas, to join
the tribe of Sisyphus and forge
the down-Underworld of Britain?
But you, convicted of your dream
to be the laureate of your nation,
transported yourself to a realm
beyond the Blue Mountains
and discovered … not 'China'—
the Shangri-La of convict fantasies—
but a dawn sky, *trees moist with dew*
and glinting all with a dim silveriness;
or the sinuous valley of the waters;
or wide warm fields, glad with corn.
You knew that nature had a sacred source
even as a sunbeam's fountain is the sun
and tried to open people's eyes.
But all they saw was a fool of God,
a voice de-crying in the wilderness,
soul-dwarfing priesthoods
and prone to drink, self-pity—yet seeing
deep down into the life of things:
and *what is deep is holy, and must tend*
to some divinely universal end.

Sham age, government, friends—
anywhere but Eurobodalla
seemed a blessing in the end.
I picture your deathbed tableau,
the spectral figure of Despair,
head bowed, pretending to grieve;
but Mary, too, sitting there
recalling your courtship; and shelves
of unread pages, hibernating
like winter trees, to open
somewhere in a future spring,
in leaf again.

Windsor is small and low-rise, spreading out from the spine of its short, modern, pedestrianised high street. But here and there lurk early Victorian gems, with lacy ironwork and balconies. There is also the Hawkesbury River, bordering the town to the north, which was part of the early formation of Charles's imagination. We walk down and see its coil of waters, broad and glaucous, slipping between banks lined with bushes and trees. I can imagine Charles, as a youngster, jumping in for a swim, or sitting on a bank, fishing. Later in his life, the river became an almost mystical conduit to his inner world, or a consoling mirror of memory. In his poem 'Dream of a Fountain' his poetic Muse appears to him and reassures him of her presence from his earliest days when he took refuge in the river:

'I am the Muse of the evergreen Forest,
I am the Spouse of thy spirit, lone Bard!
Even in the days when thy boyhood thou worest
Thy pastimes drew on thee my fondest regard.

For I felt thee even wildly, wondrously musing
Of glory and grace by old Hawkesbury's side.'

*

In his poem 'Old Billowy Hawkesb'ry', Charles returns to the river of his youth, which is now a symbol of innocent childhood compared to his present ennui: 'Ah, then could I mark in thy blue flowing billow / A vision-flushed face with no hint of a furrow ...' He confides in the river that the girl he once courted by its banks has married another man, and that his school friends, with whom he used to go swimming, have disappeared from his life. Yet the river is still a powerful current of memory and imagination:

> 'The soul of the past seems to breathe in thy cadence,
> Imparting a gush of the fiery allegiance
> I dreamt unto Glory when near thee before.'

The main physical site of contact with Charles is St Matthew's Church, on the edge of town, where he was baptised. We drive there and park by the local sportsground, which is called 'Don't Worry Oval'.

The church has a New England feel to it, with an elegant clock tower and walls composed of small red bricks.

Inside we discover a wedding ceremony crystallising, smartly dressed people fussing around, bouquets of flowers being arranged. At the back of the church is a mysterious door to something called the 'Crying Room'; we guess it's an Anglican confessional, but a church warden tells us it's a room equipped with toys and books for parents to deposit their children if they start wailing during a service. Perhaps the 'Quiet Room', or 'Consoling Room' would have a better ring to it?

I stroll around the church interior, trying to imagine Joseph Harpur and his wife Sarah, a teenage convict from Somerset, entering with their infant and taking up positions by the font. It's hard to picture Charles as a baby, knowing him only from a late photograph, showing a gaunt figure with a high forehead, unkempt thin hair, a beard reaching down to his chest.

The wedding guests are starting to filter in, so we go outside and see a white stretch-limo disgorging half a dozen Asian bridesmaids, dressed in lavender, and an Asian bride with a long white train. Sarah tells me many Chinese, Koreans and other Asians regard Australia as an exotic wedding destination. Exotic wedding destination—what would Joseph Harpur and his fellow convicts ever have thought of that?

> Windsor's old church:
> bride future-rapt!
> Chauffeur checking his watch.

We leave Windsor for the Blue Mountains and soon ascend into the foothills. It's clear from the start we're in the midst of proper mountains, a vast forested range the size of the Pyrenees.

We climb higher and higher through road shadows of sunstruck trees, then eventually branch off onto a side road and descend to a plain and a place called Killagong, which seems to be just an outdoor tea room set among trees in the middle of nowhere. But what a tea room! It's late afternoon and beyond the compound of the tables and chairs, long broad fields stretch away to a fringe of trees, behind which rise mountains. The sinking sun is mellowing the light. We gaze in a reverie, wondering whether a wallaby or two might venture forth from cover during the witching hour.

I feel as if I could stay forever; the air is a pleasant blood temperature; and we are exchanging the inner stories beneath our outer stories, something the atmosphere encourages.

Loathe to leave Arcadia, we are nevertheless conscious of having to press on in order not to be too late for Marian's house-leaving party.

Night is beginning to fall. Although we need to keep driving, we can't resist two famous look-outs en route. The first is staggering, like the Grand Canyon—a sheer cliff from which other sheer cliffs range away, descending to buckled slopes, dense with dark green trees. The panorama from the second look-out is too dark to penetrate, but the nearby pinnacles of rock known as the 'three sisters', lit by strategically placed lights, glow like angels.

> Killagong tea room:
> chairs on tables,
> fields rising with the moon.

By the time we arrive back in Annandale it's 9 pm, and Sarah has had six hours of driving, which would be enough to confine me to a hot bath for the evening. But she is made of sterner stuff.

We put on party frocks and take a taxi to Marian's place, a solid-looking period town house at the end of a mews. The party is in full swing, thirty to forty people, many of them connected with the film world: a costume designer in the corner, a script writer by the nibbles table, a casting director on the couch (not auditioning). I don't know a soul, and this feels unexpectedly liberating; I can ricochet off people, float between them, join conversations then drift away, like a waiter with a tray of badinage.

The least likely-looking bonding companion is a tall man called Paul, who has the bearing of an old rock star, with straggly longish hair and trendy red shirt and groovy shoes. He turns out to be English—he tells me he is a working-class lad from Orpington who'd got into Cambridge to read economics and, before you could say John Maynard Keynes, became an investment banker. He is the first investment banker I've met face to face, and I am his first poet. We stare at each other in wonder. And, since we are of the same vintage, we quickly bond over 1970s culture, music and soccer teams.

The party is a huge success, a last joyful and sad hurrah for Marian before she has to leave and let strangers take permanent occupation of her bedroom and cook strange food in her kitchen.

We leave late, just before we lose the will to move.

> O late-night taxi driver,
> take me home,
> tuck me up in bed!

Chord

Sunday, my last full day in Sydney and Australia. I'm taking Sarah and Alexi to the Opera House for an early afternoon concert of Bach and Haydn.

We spend the morning slouching at home, reconstructing the day before, from Windsor to Marian's party.

Just after lunch we drive to the maze of tree-lined driveways that lace the area of the Royal Botanic Garden and manage to find a parking space. We walk down to the harbour's edge, emerging from trees to a dazzle of water lapping gently at the edge. The path leads us along the margin of the sea to the Opera House, with its architectural shells tumbling forward from bigger shells.

Inside, the interior space is curiously shaped and proportioned—it's like walking into a huge ear. What I didn't know was that the building houses two main auditoriums; I had always imagined it was one big cavernous theatre, like Covent Garden, La Scala or the Met.

We take our places in the larger of the two auditoriums and sit behind the Australian Chamber Orchestra. After a deluge of clapping, they launch into the first of two short Haydn symphonies followed by various pieces of Bach.

> Bach's concerto—
> violin notes—
> sparks from a bonfire!

The players are young, dressed in black shirts worn carefully-casually outside their trousers, and the violinists are standing rather than sitting, swaying with the rhythm, giving an informal urgency to the music.

After the concert, in evening sunshine, we walk through the central harbour area to the Rocks, the oldest part of Sydney. I had always imagined this to comprise … just actual rocks and nothing else, limestone cliffs embedded with the odd fossilised shipwreck; but the area is a gentrified acropolis of small streets, markets and restaurants. There is a Sunday gentleness in the air, the phoney war before Monday.

On the way back we stop off at Marian's place so that I can say a final goodbye. Her charming cousin Siobhan is there, a gifted Melbourne sculptor, and she amuses us with a tale of the late great British poet Ted Hughes, a hero of mine, who happened to be a friend of her nanny, back in the day. She remembers coming home after a wisdom tooth operation and feeling sore, swollen-cheeked and extremely sorry for herself. Ted was there and, hearing her whimpering, dived into the fridge, grabbed two freezing tins of rice, and thrust them at her and said: 'Here, shove these against your cheeks,' and stomped out of the room. An old Yorkshire remedy, no doubt.

As we chat away, sitting outside in the small central courtyard, the sky suddenly becomes preternaturally dark. Our faces grow shadowy and the conversation falters …

> Lightning—
> seconds flicker the room …
> where is the thunder?

Leaving on a jet plane

Monday. We have to rise early to get to the airport. I'm fretful about getting stuck in traffic; Sarah is calm.

We get there in plenty of time and have a coffee, last chat, then warm hugs …

> Leaving Australia:
> how many farewells
> can a country give me?

The plane takes off and within minutes Australia has become invisible.

Feeling emotionally fragile, I chat uninhibitedly to the New Zealand woman next to me, who is going to Singapore for the first time to have a holiday with her daughter and grandchildren, resident in Melbourne. I try to present Singapore in its best light, and do a fair job of it. She tells me she is so hungry that 'right now I could give an arm and a leg for a steak', a statement that sounds almost reversible.

I distract myself by watching two Westerns, which have easily identifiable goodies and baddies, the way I like them. Towards the end of the flight I switch to flight information and there again is my favourite instruction: 'Time to SIN'.

In Singapore I'm an old hand at the shuttle-bus. Soon I'm back at my old hotel and there's my Indian receptionist friend, who recognises me immediately and smiles and points at my hat, which, this time,

I have worn especially for him. 'Hello, Mr Harpur, nice to have you back sir, and your cool hat, sir.' I tip my hat to him.

I'm too tired to walk to Killiney Road and the restaurant I went to before, so I settle for a nearby apartment store and its basement food emporium, a complex of different types of restaurants and cafés, all open-plan and running into one another.

My choice is a Thai place, efficient, spotless, but unappetising to the soul, and I'm not inclined to linger. I am struck by how different I feel compared with when I first arrived in Singapore a month ago; how quickly the excitement of being so far southeast in the world has diminished.

Next day I set off for Singapore airport early. The taxi driver is as chatty as the one I had previously, but at least he has two working arms. He can sense my anxiety about being stuck in rush-hour traffic and naturally rises to the occasion: 'You know, sir, the plane—never waits for anyone—never!' (lots of laughter). We get there in good time.

The flight to Dubai is uneventful, the plane half full, and I begin watching a nine-hour documentary about the American Civil War. I used to be a Civil War enthusiast, and I feel myself getting moist-eyed at different points in the story. I'd forgotten how fate seemed to constantly intervene in the strangest of ways. Our lives are radically changed by seemingly random meetings or events, but which take on, in retrospect, a sense of meaningful inevitability. If I hadn't entered the Vincent Buckley prize, the number of places I wouldn't have seen, and people I wouldn't have met …

Fate: In the Civil War, the first battle, Bull Run, was fought in July 1861 and centred on a farmhouse owned by a man called Wilmer McLean. After the battle, McLean thought enough was enough and moved 120 miles away to a tiny community in northern Virginia called Appomattox Court House, a place far removed from the theatres of war. The war eventually ended in April 1865, when General Robert E. Lee surrendered the Confederate army to General Ulysses

S. Grant. The place they chose to formalise the surrender was … Appomattox; and of course the actual house they randomly chose to sign the documents in was McLean's. He himself was later supposed to have said: 'The war began in my front yard and ended in my front parlor.' Coincidence? If not, what?

I continue watching the Civil War during the ongoing flight to London, and I'm caught up in the battle of Gettysburg when there's an announcement by a stewardess, asking: 'Is there a doctor on board, one of the passengers is not well.' No one moves. We are near Bucharest and I wonder whether we might have to land there. The announcement is repeated, but still no one jumps to his or her feet. We all look around, trying to locate the poor wretch. It turns out to be a young man, a few rows down from me, who looks pale and is being cared for by the staff. In the end he seems to rally, or rally enough to keep us on our flight path.

In my end is my beginning

By the time I reach London it is 8 pm, local time. I take the tube to Acton Town. I'm jet-lagged, and too many images are jostling for oxygen: Penelope at the darkened platypus enclosure in Healesville; Kevin riding off on his bike on the morning of my departure; Sappho in her basket; Sarah cooking in her kitchen; the haunted Brit in Melbourne who kept saying, 'I didn't mean to kill her'; and so it goes on.

My month of writing quietly in a backyard now seems the delusion of a fool, and thank goodness it didn't come to pass. Never in the field of writing have I met so many people of so many different types, expressing such bonhomie and kindness, and in so many different settings, in such a short time.

Cavafy expresses how I feel, in his poem 'Ithaca'. If adapted, the opening stanza might sound like this:

> As you set out for Australia
> hope your journey lasts long
> and is full of adventures and discoveries.
> Crocodiles and redbacks,
> cane toads—don't be afraid of them:
> you'll never encounter them
> if you maintain noble, dignified thoughts,
> and the excitement of exploration
> invigorates your mind and body.
> Crocodiles and redbacks,

cane toads —you won't encounter them
unless you bring them inside your soul,
and your soul displays them in front of you.

I brought them inside my mind, but perhaps not my soul.

When I get out at Acton Town, the full moon is hanging low in the sky, waiting for me in all her beauty, the same as she was four weeks ago, but somehow … not the same.

Returning home—
an ivory moon
mirrors the world—
where's Australia?

Epilogue

Three years after my return from Australia, an email arrived from Yol in early 2020:

Hi James

It's been a long time since we emailed and we hope all is well and the corona virus hasn't descended on Ireland. Are you in lock down over there? We virtually are here in Melbourne and the strange apocalyptic sense we all felt as 2020 dawned—with bush fires and floods, a billion animals wiped out and the earth's most toxic air hanging over Melbourne—hasn't improved. Alas!

We have sad news.

On Tuesday we had to have our gentle puss Sappho euthanised— thankfully here at home with us cuddling her.

We're feeling so sad and can't quite believe she's gone. She was a beautiful little creature.

And in a strange bit of serendipity, Kevin has just sent on your account of your Vincent Buckley trip to Australia, with many references to her. I've only ready the first few pages, but you've got her down pat and it's a joy to read!! Thank you for that!

Here's to Sappho and all the love she gave for those eighteen years. We're glad you got to meet her.

We hope you're all safe and healthy wherever you are, and would enjoy to hear your news.

All the best,
Yol & David

Then an email arrived from David, just after Yol's:

Hi James,

I was waiting until I had at least started your memoir before I wrote to you and I now am well into it …

As you have gathered we've had a tough week after losing Sappho. We have been comforted by your descriptions of her.

I, too have been looking at the photos and was struck, actually, by your poem about the possum at Kevin and Andrea's place. There are countless photos of Sappho in a curled position, but the one from the day before her demise are linked to your possum poem:

> Backyard Sappho
> asleep in a ball
> still a day from death

Hope you don't mind my adaptation.

Fitzroy is not a bit like the time you were here. Brunswick Street is empty with only IGA and Coles and the odd bakery open for business. (I imagine tumbleweeds rolling down the streets soon.) I was out walking early this morning and was passed by empty trams along Gertrude and Smith streets and this, at what so recently, was peak hour.

Anyway, it's great to hear from you and to be touch.

Stay well,

David and Yol

www.ingramcontent.com/pod-product-compliance
Lightning Source LLC
Chambersburg PA
CBHW030942090426
42737CB00007B/506